PRAISE FOR *RADICAL RESPONSIBILITY*

"At once inspiring and practical, this book masterfully shows us how to thrive in the face of adversity. Based on insights from ancient wisdom traditions, modern neuroscience, contemporary psychology, and his own remarkable journey from maximum-security prison inmate to transformative teacher, Fleet Maull provides a wealth of accessible tools anyone can use to discover their own basic goodness and engage more fruitfully in the world. With warmth, skill, and humility, he provides step-by-step instructions to help us courageously face reality, heal our wounds, and live richer, happier, more fulfilled, and effective lives."

RONALD D. SIEGEL, PSYD
assistant professor of psychology at Harvard Medical School
and author of *The Mindfulness Solution: Everyday
Practices for Everyday Problems*

"I've been teaching about the importance of looking at everything through the lens of personal responsibility for decades. Taking personal responsibility is the only 'above the line' perspective. Anything else—blaming, shaming, or justifying—is decidedly 'below the line,' and will only hold you back and limit your opportunities for advancement and growth. Fleet addresses this issue beautifully in *Radical Responsibility*, and I wholeheartedly endorse his work."

MARSHALL THURBER
cofounder of Burklyn, student of Buckminster Fuller
and W. Edwards Deming, and creator of *Money and You*®

"This important work by Fleet Maull is full of practical wisdom and is written from his deep experience as a teacher, practitioner, and guide of corporate executives, chaplains, and those serving others. It is a rare treasure and a book for today and for all time."

ROSHI JOAN HALIFAX, PHD
abbot of Upaya Zen Center and author of *Standing at the
Edge: Finding Freedom Where Fear and Courage Meet*

"*Radical Responsibility* is an empowering and heartfelt guidebook to living more fully, a systematic training for practical liberation in your life."

JACK KORNFIELD, PHD
author of *A Path with Heart*

"This is one of the most powerful books I've ever read. With great clarity and heart, it combines brain science, psychology, and soulful wisdom to help readers grow inner strength and inner peace. Fleet Maull is a friendly guide—someone who has seen both the worst of life and its highest possibilities, and who brings gritty good humor, deep insight, and practical suggestions to every page."

RICK HANSON, PHD
author of *Resilient: How to Grow an Unshakable
Core of Calm, Strength, and Happiness*

"It's a rare privilege to read the work of someone who walks the talk as fully as Fleet Maull. The transforming wisdom of his extraordinary life experience—from dharma practitioner to prison inmate to spiritual mentor—suffuses every page of this wonderful book. Engaging, pragmatic, and deeply insightful, *Radical Responsibility* shows us all how to take responsibility for the habit patterns of our lives. With personal stories, psychological research, and a range of meditative exercises, Fleet illuminates the possibilities of living a freer and more joyful life. Highly recommended."

JOSEPH GOLDSTEIN
author of *Mindfulness: A Practical Guide to Awakening*

"Fleet Maull has lived a life of transformation. Emerging from a drama-filled life that led to imprisonment, he knows deeply what I call the 'Dreaded Drama Triangle'—originally the Karpman Drama Triangle—and its roles of Victim, Persecutor, and Rescuer. His journey of awakening to his essence as a Creator should be an inspiration to all. He is an exemplar of TED* (*The Empowerment Dynamic®), and through *Radical Responsibility*, he serves as a Challenger and Coach to readers to become Creators in their own lives."

DAVID EMERALD (WOMELDORFF)
author of *The Power of TED** (*The Empowerment Dynamic)

"Following the path of *Radical Responsibility*—a gift to us from author Fleet Maull's amazing real-life backstory—we learn to own our choices and create the freedom to craft our lives to be truly happy, reach our highest potential, and be a force for good that can change the world."

SHARON SALZBERG
author of *Real Happiness* and *Real Love*

"Fleet Maull draws on his unique life journey and remarkable expertise, sharing with us how we can find equanimity and compassion in the maelstrom of our days. *Radical Responsibility* offers a sound and original blueprint for a life well lived."

DANIEL GOLEMAN
author of *Emotional Intelligence*

"A practical, direct, and accessible guide to human flourishing from someone who faced tremendous adversity and emerged from this challenge with vigor, equanimity, and the deepest passion to share his wisdom for the benefit of others. This book is a gift for anyone facing adversity, which is all of us!"

RICHARD J. DAVIDSON, PHD
coauthor of *The Emotional Life of Your Brain* and *Altered Traits*;
founder and director, Center for Healthy Minds,
University of Wisconsin-Madison

"Fleet Maull's creative and time-tested framework for reining in your own mind's inflammatory, self-destructive, imprisoning tendencies can be powerfully freeing—and healing. All you need to do is put it into practice. He guides you in exactly how to do that and sustain it for life. You couldn't be in better hands or have a more capable and authentic guide."

JON KABAT-ZINN, PHD
author of *Full Catastrophe Living*
and *Mindfulness for All*

"The path of *Radical Responsibility* evolves our capacity to respond—with wisdom, courage, and love—to the suffering of our world. Author Fleet Maull guides us masterfully in awakening from our separateness and inspires a profound dedication to caring for ourselves and each other."

TARA BRACH, PHD
author of *Radical Acceptance* and *True Refuge*

RADICAL
RESPONSIBILITY

ALSO BY FLEET MAULL

Dharma in Hell: The Prison Writings of Fleet Maull

RADICAL RESPONSIBILITY

HOW TO MOVE BEYOND BLAME, FEARLESSLY LIVE YOUR HIGHEST PURPOSE, AND BECOME AN UNSTOPPABLE FORCE FOR GOOD

A Mindfulness-Based Emotional Intelligence Guide for Personal Evolution, Self-Actualization, and Social Transformation

FLEET MAULL, PHD

sounds true
BOULDER, COLORADO

Sounds True
Boulder, CO 80306

This book is not intended as a substitute for the medical recommendations of physicians,
mental health professionals, or other health-care providers. Rather, it is intended to offer
information to help the reader cooperate with physicians, mental health professionals,
and health-care providers in a mutual quest for optimal well-being. We advise readers to
carefully review and understand the ideas presented and to seek the advice of a qualified
professional as is necessary.

Published 2019

Book design by Beth Skelley

Printed in Canada

Library of Congress Cataloging-in-Publication Data
Names: Maull, Fleet, author.
Title: Radical responsibility : how to move beyond blame, fearlessly live
    your highest purpose, and become an unstoppable force for good / Fleet Maull, PhD.
Description: Boulder, CO : Sounds True, 2019.
Identifiers: LCCN 2018044451 (print) | LCCN 2018046568 (ebook) |
    ISBN 9781683641964 (ebook) | ISBN 9781683641698 (hardcover)
Subjects: LCSH: Self-actualization (Psychology) | Change (Psychology) |
    Emotional intelligence. | Mindfulness (Psychology) | Social change.
Classification: LCC BF637.S4 (ebook) | LCC BF637.S4 M3825 2019 (print) |
    DDC 155.2—dc23
LC record available at https://lccn.loc.gov/2018044451

10 9 8 7 6 5 4 3 2 1

I dedicate this book to my beloved parents, Lou and Pat Maull, inveterate readers who I wish were alive to read this work, and to my son, Robert, who has continually inspired my efforts to make a positive contribution to this world of ours. I also dedicate this book to my late partner, Denise Thornton, who died entirely too young from cancer in 2008 and who continually encouraged me to "write the book!" Finally, I would like to dedicate this work to my teacher Chögyam Trungpa Rinpoche and his vision for creating an enlightened society.

CONTENTS

🔊)) *Audio versions of the exercises marked with this icon can be streamed or downloaded at SoundsTrue.com/store/rrpractices*

LIST OF FIGURES

FOREWORD

We are at a time in human development that invites us to consider becoming leaders in bringing more well-being not only to our inner, personal lives but also to the larger world in which we live. We all breathe the same air, share the same sources of water and food, and even have a common evolutionary history as part of an extended human family. This book offers powerful insights into the practical steps you can take to strengthen your mind in science-backed ways that can help you participate in the pervasive leadership needed to take responsibility for your inner and collective well-being in this shared journey of life.

Fleet Maull's personal journey of incarceration and reflection serves as the experiential bedrock for deep learning that has inspired his working life to focus on the well-being of others and their liberation from that all-too-common automatic-pilot way of living that imprisons so many of us in a mental cage of our own creation. Born from this background, *Radical Responsibility* is a brilliant travel guide that invites you to take in the hard-earned lessons from a teacher who serves as a companion along the important journey of waking up your mind to a vital way of living in our world.

We have a choice. The mind can function on autopilot, carrying out information processes without much awareness, reflexively reacting to what life dishes out, and behaving in ways more informed by what we've learned in our personal lives or inherited from a long evolution of threat and survival strategies. Or we can learn the steps necessary to wake up our awareness to become "radically responsible" for our inner lives and our interactive actions. Waking up in this way is itself a radical act of realizing that we can each be responsible for the growth of our mind and the interactions we have with others in the world. When we take on that leadership role, the world can be changed one person, one relationship, one interaction at a time.

To achieve such a radical change in our collective lives, our guide has skillfully provided a compelling balance of conceptual ideas, illuminating stories, and practical exercises to cultivate a more open awareness that is the gateway to living life wide awake and learning to behave in ways that promote well-being in our inner and relational worlds. You may already be familiar with some of these steps, or they may be quite new to your way of thinking. Whether you are experienced or a novice in training your mind, this book invites you on a growth-promoting journey that will enhance your understanding and your way of being in the world.

How can developing the mind change our lives? Our mind is both an internal process and an "inter" process—one that is within our body and between the body and the world around us. Energy and information flow happen in this within-and-between location of who we are. When that flow is integrated—when it is differentiated and linked—it optimizes how it functions. This self-organizing aspect of the mind means that if you can learn to liberate the mind's natural push toward integration from its all-too-common slumber, then your life, within and between, can become more flexible, adaptive, coherent (resilient over time), energized, and stable. When this happens inside of us, we can experience a sense of freedom and clarity in our awareness. When this happens between our inner self and the world around us, including our interpersonal relationships, we bring more empathy, compassion, and kindness into the world.

When created in a repeated way, these integrated states in the moment can become traits of integration in the long run. This movement from states to traits happens because of the simple axiom "Where attention goes, neural firing flows, and neural connection grows." An awakening mind is an integrating mind that changes the structure of the brain itself in integrative ways. The science behind this is fascinating, and the steps supporting such growth of optimal regulation of attention, emotion, thought, behavior, memory, and ethical responsibility each emerge from a more integrated functional and structural set of changes in the brain itself. Yes, this is a radical idea: your mind can change the structure of your brain. When those changes are linking different parts to one another, when they are integrating, optimal living emerges.

Research is quite clear: training the mind to focus attention, open awareness, and cultivate kind intention and compassion creates a more integrated brain and gives rise to an awakened mind as we foster well-being in our lives. The radical act of reading this book to generate this kind of responsible way of living is a step toward being a leader in your own life and bringing more connection, respect, and well-being into the world. Are you ready to dive in? Join Fleet on a journey into becoming a leader in our world that starts from the inside out. Enjoy!

Daniel J. Siegel, MD

Mindsight Institute
Author, *Aware: The Science
and Practice of Presence*

ACKNOWLEDGMENTS

would like to thank Danielle Wolffe for providing invaluable assistance in the early stages of transcribing my seminars and developing a structure for this book. I especially want to thank my sweetheart and partner, Sophie Leger. Without her loving support and expert editing, I could not possibly have completed this book. I want to offer special thanks to my agent, David Nelson, at Waterside Productions, who has believed in this work from the outset. I also wish to thank the team at Sounds True—especially Tami Simon, Jennifer Brown, and my editor, Robert Lee—for their skillful guidance and unflagging encouragement.

I would like to offer special acknowledgment and profound gratitude to my dearest friend and spiritual brother, Purna Steinitz, who first introduced me to the core context underlying this work through The Event, a transformational training I had the privilege of co-leading with Purna for more than fifteen years. I would also like to express deep gratitude to a fellow ex-prisoner, Ken Windes, who cofounded The Game (precursor to The Event), and to his mentors Dr. Martin Groder and Marshall Thurber.

Finally, I want to express my profound gratitude to the various spiritual teachers, mentors, and friends who have guided and inspired my journey these many years, including Chögyam Trungpa Rinpoche, Roshi Bernie Glassman, Roshi Sandra Jishu Holmes, Pema Chödrön, Roshi Joan Halifax, and Lee Lozowick. I especially want to thank my longtime colleagues and "co-conspirators" Kate Crisp and Roshi Grover Genro Guantt, for their support, friendship, and contributions to my journey and this work. Throughout the fifteen-year journey of bringing this book to completion, Trungpa Rinpoche's echoing encouragement ("You can do it!") kept me from throwing in the towel in even the most despairing moments.

INTRODUCTION

My primary purpose in writing this book is to place in your hands the same insights, distinctions, and tools I used to dramatically transform my own life from a long night's passage in an isolation cell facing a possible life sentence to a successful, exciting, and deeply rewarding international career as a meditation teacher, business consultant, seminar leader, and social entrepreneur. Perhaps more to the heart of the matter, these are the same tools through which I discovered my own integrity, self-discipline, authenticity, and personal freedom.

In 1985, I spent a sleepless night in a suicide-watch isolation cell, pondering and dreading my fate: the possibility of being sentenced to life without parole. I was not suicidal but, anticipating my sentence later that morning, I was in a highly anxious and agitated state. My life as I knew it was over. I was thirty-five years old, well educated, with talent and potential, and I had completely torched my life—burned it to the ground. My nine-year-old son, who would now grow up without a father, had returned, penniless, to South America with his mother. My assets had all been confiscated and debts were piling up. My family and friends were suffering, frightened, confused, and in some cases justifiably angry.

I had been convicted of *continuous criminal enterprise*, the so-called kingpin statute, for smuggling cocaine from South America to the United States. This carried with it a no-parole sentence of ten years to life in prison. At that time, prior to 1987, parole still existed in the federal system. I was guilty of smuggling, and I would have pled guilty if it were not for the kingpin charge, which I felt at the time was a punishment for refusing to inform or testify against others. The jury convicted me on all counts. Given the media attention my trial received, I knew my sentence would not be minimal.

Desperate for relief from the claustrophobia of that tomb-like cell, I stood on the stainless steel toilet and sink to peer out the one small window at the night sky and stars. As dawn began to break, I shifted from extreme desperation and anxiety to a calm, peaceful resolve. I had decided deep in my being that no matter what sentence I received later that morning, I would not give up. I would not give up on life, my son, or myself. Never. This book is the result of the journey that began early that morning.

Standing before the judge, my knees buckled as he pronounced my sentence—thirty years with no possibility of parole. My lawyer kept me from falling. I had secretly been hoping, maybe praying, for fifteen or twenty. As the US Marshals escorted me back to the holding cell, I shoved down the tears and stifled a sob. I'd seen the marshals make fun of other prisoners for crying; I'd be damned if I'd give them that pleasure. Later that night, sleepless in another county jail cell, I desperately wanted the tears to flow, but I'd lost them. Jail is no place for tears.

This book is not about me; it's about you.

I went through a classic "dark night of the soul" over the weeks to come as I awaited transfer to a federal prison. I was devastated by the sober realization of what I had done to myself and my family and the tough journey that lay ahead, but most of all by what I had done to my son, Robert, who would now grow up with his father in prison. The headline in the newspaper the next day read something like, "Drug Kingpin Maull Sentenced to 30 Years Without Parole; Will Be 65 Years Old Before He Can Be Released." As I considered what lay ahead, I made a crystal-clear, radical commitment to eradicate all negativity from my life and somehow use my education and talents to accomplish something of value during my time in prison, something that might allow my son to hold his head up and be proud of his dad.

I knew in the depth of my being that continuing my meditation practice would be the foundation, not only for surviving but also for anything positive I could hope to accomplish. With ten years of training under my belt, I knew what to do. I began practicing several hours every night, sitting on the top bunk in a two-person cell in that steel-and-concrete tomb of a county jail, amid the echoing cacophony of blaring televisions and radios, prisoners trading war stories, and the screaming from the other tanks, where they held state prisoners and local drunks. Late one night as I sat in meditation, focused on my breathing, well aware of all the noise and chaos around me, I realized that my mind was not moving at all. It was not reacting to all the jarring sounds. I felt complete clarity, peace, and serenity. I had experiences like this during previous meditation retreats, but never in this kind of crazy environment. At that moment I felt a strong assurance that I could do this prison thing. I was still terrified, still having nightmares about being attacked or raped; but somehow that night, meditating on that upper bunk, I found an unshakable confidence in the depths of my being that has remained unshakable to this day.

This is not a prison memoir. That book remains to be written another day. And this book is not about me; it's about you—it's a manual for your own personal evolution and self-actualization. Within these pages you'll receive everything I learned during fourteen years in a maximum security prison, in addition to everything I've learned since. In the twenty years since my release, I've been offering some form of this material through trainings to thousands of business leaders, prisoners, correctional officers, law enforcement officials, and members of the general public. I'm now very inspired to offer the complete Radical Responsibility model for the first time, having worked on it and lived it to the best of my ability for the past thirty-three years. My humble aspiration is that this book will fulfill its promise and support you in moving beyond blame to fearlessly live your highest purpose and become an unstoppable force for good.

One of my goals is that you become what best-selling author and life coach Tony Robbins calls a "practical psychologist," someone who understands enough about human behavior to navigate life with less drama and heartache and a great deal more creativity, joy, and fulfillment.[1] Though I landed in prison with a master's degree in psychology (and have since earned my doctorate), I earned my practical psychologist credentials on the job, so to speak, during my stay in a maximum security prison, which taught me how to work with people and better understand myself. Maximum security prisons are what sociologists call *total institutions*, essentially totalitarian environments where the staff and administrators have absolute authority and control, and resistance is literally futile. If you tried to significantly buck the system there, you'd end up in four-point restraints on a concrete bunk in one of the psych wards, injected with antipsychotics such as Haldol or Thorazine, and getting hosed down at night.

So how do you get anything done in such an environment, much less create significant change? If you ask the prison staff for anything new or different, the answer is always no, followed by some version of "We had a program like that, but the inmates abused it, so we got rid of it." For me, the answer was remembering that everyone, even the most hardened correctional officers or prison administrators, were human beings. I learned that if I was patient, compassionate, and respectful, sooner or later I would find a way to approach someone who would open doors to new possibilities.

Radical Responsibility is a shame-free philosophy that transcends blame.

Taking this approach, I initiated numerous programs at the United States Medical Center for Federal Prisoners in Springfield, Missouri, the maximum security prison hospital where I served my time. Such programs included a variety of personal growth programs, one of the first inside-prison hospice programs anywhere in the world, and two national organizations—Prison Mindfulness Institute (PMI) and National Prison Hospice Association (NPHA). Today, PMI trains teachers and facilitators all around the world to bring mindfulness to at-risk, incarcerated, and reentering youth and adults, as well as correctional officers, law enforcement personnel, judges, prosecutors, public defenders, probation and parole officers, and treatment providers. The PMI network includes more than 180 organizations and projects that bring mindfulness and contemplative spirituality to our jails, prisons, and juvenile facilities, with thousands of individual volunteers doing the same. NPHA has played a key role in catalyzing and building a prison hospice movement that now includes over seventy-five prison hospice programs in US state and federal prisons. I highlight all of this not to pat myself on the back, but rather to illustrate what is possible through Radical Responsibility, even in the most challenging and seemingly powerless circumstances.

My more universal purpose is to help people gain freedom from the disempowering, traumatizing, and ultimately demeaning scourge of blame and shame that dominates our Western culture. All of this arises from the perverse notion that human beings are somehow ultimately flawed and even dangerous. Radical Responsibility is a shame-free philosophy that transcends blame. It's a practical approach to life grounded in the historically predominant, cross-cultural consensus that human beings are innately good and that all of life is inherently sacred. Radical Responsibility is also the conscious choice to fully empower ourselves by embracing 100 percent responsibility for each and every circumstance we face in life, free of even a hint of self-blame. How is this possible? Someone must be to blame when bad things happen, when injustices occur, right? What about all those people committing heinous acts and truly victimizing others? I can only encourage you to read on.

This book arises out of a profound compassion for the endless suffering we have visited upon each other as human beings, and I aspire that not one more child or adult be traumatized by neglect, abuse, violence, oppression, racism, marginalization, poverty, genocide, war, or refugee crises. *Radical Responsibility* addresses the very core of our human condition where the possibilities of imprisonment and freedom, violence and peace, suffering and joy continuously co-arise, offering us the same alternative repeatedly: either awaken to the liberating power of conscious ownership or give power away by blaming others and abdicating responsibility for our choices. The distinction between blame and ownership is the most critical distinction offered in this book. My core message is that by embracing Radical Responsibility for the choices we make, we discover the fruits of self-empowerment and genuine personal freedom, and that we can do so with profound self-compassion, completely free of self-blame. In doing so, Radical Responsibility empowers us to effectively make boundaries, speak truth to power, prevent harm, and promote healing and transformation for all.

This book is organized into five parts. In part I, we will explore the basic context and foundational skills for the path of Radical

Responsibility: unconditional human goodness and mindfulness-based emotional intelligence (MBEI). In part II, we will take a deep dive into the challenges of the human condition in order to see with clarity, insight, and compassion how we got to where we are and how we continue to perpetuate confusion and suffering for ourselves and others. In part III, we will explore the physiology, psychology, and neurobiology of change and transformation and how to take charge of our destiny and step into the driver's seat (or at least the copilot's seat) of our own lives. In part IV, we experientially journey through the core of Radical Responsibility, directly experiencing the fundamental shift from blame to ownership, the key transformative distinction on this journey. In part V, we will discover the extraordinary capacities and wisdom of the heart-mind and then be guided to create our own, deeply-considered life plan in order to realize the promise of this book.

This book includes a number of exercises and guided meditations. Please acquire a journal or notebook and keep it close at hand while reading this book. I will regularly invite you to participate in reflective exercises that involve writing. I will also invite you to develop a regular mindfulness practice with plenty of support and instruction. To get the greatest benefit from *Radical Responsibility*, please complete all the exercises and practice the meditations again and again. We all know there is a direct relationship between our level of engagement and what we get out of any learning or training experience, so please jump in wholeheartedly.

Those of you who have attended my live or online Radical Responsibility seminars might wonder why some aspects aren't included in this book. Suffice it to say that the constraints of the written word led me to choose the most essential aspects of those trainings to include here, and I'm quite inspired by the result. I encourage you to just jump in—I promise you won't be disappointed. No matter if you're quite familiar with this work or encountering it for the first time, there's something valuable in this book for you.

So get ready to create an entirely new context for your life, one that will empower you to realize your greatest possibilities. Be sure to take your time with the foundational chapters that follow—they set the stage for quite an amazing journey.

PART I

THE BEGINNING

Innate Goodness and
Mindfulness-Based
Emotional Intelligence

In spite of all our problems and confusion, all our emotional
and psychological ups and downs, there is something basically
good about our existence as human beings. We have moments
of basic non-aggression and freshness . . . we have an actual
connection to reality that can wake us up and make us feel basically,
fundamentally good. **CHÖGYAM TRUNGPA RINPOCHE**

1

THERE'S NOTHING WRONG WITH YOU

The foundational premise of Radical Responsibility is that there
is absolutely nothing fundamentally wrong with you, or me,
or anyone else for that matter. This radical message or truth is
the good news of this book. Now the bad news: we have all been
indoctrinated, to one degree or another—through parental, religious,
educational, cultural, and media influences—with quite the opposite
message, and this indoctrination, though based on misunderstandings
and untruths, is not so easily undone. We can, however, release this
negative stranglehold with gentle effort, self-compassion, and perse-
verance. That's the second piece of good news. We can even wake up to
the truth of our innate, unconditional *basic goodness* in a flash of transformative insight. However, even after such an illumination, most of
us still have work to do, which is why human and/or spiritual development is often described as a path or journey.

That journey is what this book is all about. It begins with cultivating sufficient confidence in unconditional, innate goodness—our own
and that of others. By doing so, we can move beyond blame and other

fear-based coping strategies to embrace a radical level of ownership for each and every circumstance we encounter in life. Once we do that, we can fearlessly live our highest purpose and become an unstoppable force for good in the world.

◀)) **OPENING EXERCISE   Part 1**

Please read the following list aloud to yourself slowly, going over each line once or twice and then closing your eyes to reflect on what comes up for you before going on to the next one. Just do your best to notice whatever comes up and be with it. Remember—there are no right answers!

- There is nothing wrong with you.

- You are not broken.

- You don't need fixing.

- You are an innately and unconditionally good, whole, intelligent, and beautiful human being.

- You are basically good, whole, and okay just as you are.

- You are here for a reason.

- You are not an accident.

- The world needs you.

- You are lovable and loved.

Okay, so what came up for you? I've led this exercise in person countless times with all kinds of folks—young children, teenagers, CEOs, business professionals, prisoners, correctional officers—and they all have different experiences, all completely valid. For some, hearing these statements aloud feels relieving or validating. Others experience distrust or suspicion—"What does this guy know about me?"—or they feel a wave of unworthiness or self-criticism—"If only that were true, but I'm definitely *not* basically good." Maybe one of these responses matches your own, or maybe what came up for you was a mixed bag—some positive and some not-so-positive feelings. Whether you found these statements comforting, validating, challenging, irritating, threatening, heartbreaking, confusing, or all the above, I invite you to just honor your own experience and remember that all change, growth, and transformation happens outside our comfort zone.

◀)) **OPENING EXERCISE** **Part 2**

Let's try this again with a slight change in the wording of the statements. Just like before, read each statement aloud to yourself at least once, slowly, and then close your eyes to reflect. Or, if you prefer, read the complete list through once and then close your eyes to contemplate what comes up.

- There is nothing wrong with me.

- I am not broken.

- I don't need fixing.

- I am an innately and unconditionally good, whole, intelligent, and beautiful human being.

- I am basically good, whole, and okay just as I am.

- I am here for a reason.

- I am not an accident.

- The world needs me.

- I am lovable and loved.

Was that different from the first time around? How did it feel for you? Whatever came up for you might not feel comfortable, but it's incredibly important to see and feel. We're uncovering some of the underlying beliefs you carry around that drive your attitudes, feelings, behaviors, and—ultimately—the direction of your life and destiny. Discovering your basic core beliefs and getting clear about which ones serve you and which ones don't is the beginning of taking charge of your destiny as a human being.

Before you read on, please take a few minutes to write something about your experience with this exercise in your Radical Responsibility journal.

DISCOVERING BASIC GOODNESS

Meditation is about learning to recognize our basic goodness in the immediacy of the present moment, and then nurturing this recognition until it seeps into the very core of our being. **MINGYUR RINPOCHE**

This book—and the Radical Responsibility path itself—are grounded in the contemplative discipline of mindfulness and awareness meditation. For thousands of years, human beings in cultures all around the world have employed various meditative and introspective practices to explore the depths of our humanity, discovering again and again a dimension of being in which our innate goodness and wholeness are undeniable. By quieting the mind's chatter, mystics, contemplatives, yogis, shamans, and ordinary people have discovered a deeper dimension of being that is beyond fear and the dichotomy of good and bad—a place of experiential wholeness, strength, and resilience where ineffable peace and bliss abound. Needless to say, whenever we can touch into this dimension of our being, we experience ourselves and the world in a significantly different way.

During my years in prison, despite my inclination to believe in the basic goodness of everyone, I sometimes wondered about a few of the correctional officers and some of my fellow prisoners. My skeptical disposition led me to contemplate if it were actually possible that perhaps not *all* human beings possessed innate basic goodness. I developed an informal research project of sorts. Every time I thought I had discovered a fellow prisoner or correctional officer absent this innate goodness, they would inevitably reveal their vulnerability and basic goodness in some way. I'll never forget the moment when a correctional officer I had previously experienced as being one of the most abusive guards in the prison asked me with genuine interest how my son was doing, having seen us together in the visiting room months earlier. After several years of similar experiences, I concluded my research project, more convinced than ever of the goodness in everyone.

Trust in Allah but tether your camel.

As we begin to trust more in this unconditional basic goodness, we recognize ourselves and others as belonging to an interconnected whole, inseparable from the beauty and sacredness of the world around us—as opposed to continually dividing our experience into friends and enemies, things to be desired or avoided, blessings to accumulate or threats to ward off. And in case you're thinking that this all sounds like some kind of naïve, pie-in-the-sky spiritual optimism that's bound to set you up for disappointment or worse, I'd like to share one of my favorite aphorisms from the Sufi tradition: Trust in Allah but tether your camel. In other words, trust in the goodness and wholeness of life *while at the same time* being responsible, maintaining healthy boundaries, taking care of business, preventing problems, and promoting positive outcomes. This blend of experiential confidence in innate goodness and practical, no-nonsense personal responsibility and accountability is at the very heart of Radical Responsibility.

The next chapter offers a deep dive into the practices of mindfulness meditation, but there's no time like the present to jump in, so let's try it out. You may want to read the guided meditation below slowly to yourself and then set the book down to do the exercise. You could also have someone read it to you aloud or record it yourself in order to play it back while you learn this practice.

Radical Responsibility is not about fixing yourself.

EXERCISE   Opening Meditation

Please find a quiet moment and place where you can sit undisturbed for ten or fifteen minutes. Choose any place or seating arrangement that attracts you, whether it's a meditation cushion, your favorite chair, your living room sofa, or—weather permitting—a favorite bench in a nearby park. If you're sitting on a cushion or bench, you may want to sit up with a nicely erect, yet relaxed posture; and if you've chosen a big leather easy chair, feel free to sit back and enjoy feeling supported and relaxed, just the way these chairs are designed to enfold us in luxurious comfort.

Once settled in your spot, gently close your eyes or lower your gaze and bring your focus to your body and breathing, just noticing whatever arises for you physically in the moment. You may find yourself experiencing a range of sensations—some pleasant and comfortable, some relatively neutral, and some perhaps a bit uncomfortable and not so pleasant. Do your best to simply recognize each sensation as an experience of being alive in a human body—your body. As you focus on this dimension of sensate experience, notice and feel how your breathing and the sensations are connected. Relax into simply feeling and appreciating the flow of your breath moving in and out of your body, along with the continual flow of sensations arising and falling away, much like leaves floating in a stream or clouds passing by in the sky.

After a few minutes of appreciating this continual flow of sensate aliveness in your body and breath, gently open your eyes or raise your gaze and begin taking in the world around you. Notice whatever appears in your immediate surroundings—a favorite picture or photograph on the wall, the way light and shadow play on the objects in your immediate vicinity, or perhaps a flower, tree, or the sky above you. What are you feeling? Is there any shift in the way you are experiencing yourself and your connection to the world around you?

Please take a moment to jot down a few notes about your experience of this practice in your Radical Responsibility journal for later reflection.

I strongly recommend making a habit of taking time out for yourself in this way, setting aside quiet times for solitude, reflection, and *being-ness*. Our world is so focused on *doing* that we have lost track of the importance of *being*. We've forgotten to allow time for what children and mystics have known to do for millennia—to simply *be* and appreciate the wonder, magic, and aliveness of our immediate moment-to-moment experience.

THE JOURNEY

In this book we will explore what it means to begin a journey of discovery, transformation, and personal evolution free from the goad or lash of self-criticism and blame. This is not a self-improvement book. Radical Responsibility is not about fixing yourself. Instead, I invite you to embark on this journey with the faith and confidence that underneath all your conditioning and even your most pernicious negative habits, you are already innately and unconditionally good, pure, wise, and completely whole—just as you are. In this way, Radical Responsibility begins by compassionately allowing the clouds of misinformation and misunderstanding to dissipate so that you clearly experience the ever-present sun of basic goodness radiating forth from the depth of your being. This perspective makes all the difference.

On this very personal journey, you will establish a life context that transcends blame and any sense of being somehow inherently at fault or fundamentally mistaken. You will be free to explore, practice, struggle with, chew on, and digest the ideas, distinctions, and exercises presented here in your own way, at your own pace, with no concern whatsoever for doing it right—or wrong, for that matter. When we realize that who we are is originally good, pure, and without fault, then we are free to play and make mistakes, just as young children naturally learn best by falling down and getting up over and over again, spilling and knocking things over, and exploring their world freely, absent the threat of blame or criticism. In this way, our journey is beyond the conventional context of winning and losing, getting it right, or even achieving something. This is simply an open-hearted exploration of what it means to be human.

As we explore the notion of embracing Radical Responsibility in even the most challenging and vexing life circumstances, it is of paramount importance that we develop greater confidence in our own innate basic goodness and the basic goodness of humanity all together. It's that confidence that will foster the self-compassion, resilience, and wisdom we'll need moving forward. One of the most effective ways to build that confidence, in my opinion, is to work with tried-and-true contemplative practices from the world's wisdom traditions. These techniques have been honed for thousands of years, and they are designed to help us relax into being-ness and discover our own inherent goodness. In doing so, we come to accept and recognize the relative good, bad, and ugly of all our *stuff* as simply the beautiful and challenging legacy of our shared humanity—the human challenge that unites us all. As we relax into this natural state and empowering self-acceptance, it becomes increasingly difficult to entertain the notion that there's something fundamentally wrong with us. This pernicious untruth and misunderstanding about our human nature simply doesn't hold up any longer—thank *goodness*!

> As soon as you honor the present moment, all unhappiness
> and struggle dissolve, and life begins to flow with joy and ease.
> When you act out the present-moment awareness, whatever
> you do becomes imbued with a sense of quality, care, and
> love—even the most simple action. **ECKHART TOLLE**

2

THE POWER OF PRESENCE

Have you had the experience of driving through several major intersections and suddenly realizing you don't remember whether the lights were red or green? Most of us have. Fortunately, our brain has an autopilot function—a highly programmed supercomputer, sometimes called the *bottom-up brain*, that can perform billions of operations a minute. We all have a bit (or a lot) of the absent-minded professor in us. We have untrained and highly discursive minds, which, left to their own devices, keep us distracted much of the time. We actually spend much of our so-called waking lives lost in thought, most of it fairly inconsequential thought at that, rather than experiencing life in all its vivid texture, mystery, and power. We are essentially sleepwalking through life much of the time, immersed in one randomly arising daydream after another. No wonder sages and prophets throughout the ages have been calling us to *wake up*.

What is it that we most appreciate in others, especially those with whom we relate most closely—our spouse or partner, family members, friends, work colleagues, and so on? For most of us, it's probably the quality of their presence. When people really show up—when they listen to us and are truly available—we feel seen, heard, appreciated, and valued. Such experiences create genuine meaning and connection, so it makes sense that we would want to cultivate the ability to be truly present for others, especially those we care about and those who depend on us.

Our wild, untrained, wandering mind has been referred to as *monkey mind*, calling forth the image of a large tree in which hundreds of monkeys clamber about, swinging from branch to branch, making a cacophonous racket. Sometimes our discursive mind feels like a pinball machine, the ball randomly careening every which way, lights blinking on and off, and bells ringing; or it may feel like the worst of rush hour traffic, beeping horns, road rage and all. One of the best analogies for our wild mind is that of a runaway horse. Imagine that you, the rider, have fallen from the saddle, but one foot is stuck in the stirrup as your horse takes off at a gallop, dragging you across hill and dale, your head scraping the ground and hitting every rock, gully, and puddle. Sounds a bit like how life feels at times, doesn't it?

> Either you learn to ride the donkey or the donkey rides you.

The horse in this analogy is your conditioned mind in its wild and undisciplined state; it's been dragging you through all kinds of situations your entire life, many of which you might have preferred to avoid. In this chapter you will learn how to regain your seat in the saddle, tame the wild horse, and ride the energy of your mind, directing it to where you want to go. My first meditation teacher used to say, "Either you learn to ride the donkey or the donkey rides you."[1]

How did that go? If you are like most of us, it wasn't so easy to keep your attention on your breathing. Your mind may have wandered all over the place. You may have had all kinds of thoughts clamoring for your attention. Five minutes may have felt like five hours. You may have felt physically restless and fidgety. An itch on your face may have demanded scratching. For some of you, this five-minute exercise may have felt restful or peaceful. If you didn't experience monkey mind this time around though, try sitting still for twenty minutes or more. It will definitely show up at some point.

While we all strongly tend toward discursive thinking, distraction, and operating on autopilot, we also all know how to pay attention when the situation or activity demands it. We perform actions all the time that are impossible to do on autopilot—digging a splinter out of a child's finger or returning a tennis serve, for example. The ability to rouse our energy and direct our attention toward an object or activity is one of our most important human skills. Craftspeople, artists, musicians, dancers, athletes, and other performers all learn to train their capacity for attention. Generally, this attentiveness is directed at a specific activity, such as hitting a fastball or playing a violin, but it isn't regularly applied to the seemingly mundane activities of everyday life. For thousands of years, artists and athletes of another sort—the monastics and yogis of the world's great contemplative traditions—have recognized the need to tame our wild mind and train our attention in service of awakening to our true nature and destiny as human beings. Their practices go by many names, but we typically know them as meditation, contemplation, or yoga.

Recently, the most common term used in secular or scientific circles is *mindfulness*.

In the past few years, mindfulness has exploded into the mainstream in the United States and other Western countries, appended to just about anything we can imagine: mindful coaching, mindful yoga, mindful eating, mindfulness-based stress reduction (MBSR), mindful teaching, mindfulness-based cognitive therapy (MBCT), and the mindfulness-based emotional intelligence (MBEI) model presented in this book. Why has this ancient and universal mind-training discipline suddenly become all the rage? For one, scientific research has clearly demonstrated that a wandering mind is an unhappy mind, and that a focused, attentive mind enhances feelings of well-being and, you guessed it, happiness.[2] Research has also shown that basic mindfulness practice improves brain health and performance across almost every dimension of our brain's complex operations.[3]

But what is mindfulness exactly? Jon Kabat-Zinn, who developed MBSR, defines it as "paying attention in a particular way; on purpose, in the present moment, and nonjudgmentally."[4] Researchers G. Alan Marlatt and Jean L. Kristeller describe mindfulness as the process of "bringing one's complete attention to the present experience on a moment-to-moment basis."[5]

In mindfulness training you learn to ride the energy of the mind.

Practiced as a form of mind training in service of spiritual liberation by practitioners for millennia, the essence of formal mindfulness practice involves placing one's attention on a chosen object—the breath, the body, or an external or visualized object, for example. *Mindfulness of breathing* is a common practice found across various traditions.

While mindfulness can be practiced in any posture and with any activity, the most common position for formal mindfulness meditation training is the seated posture. Given the habitual speediness and restlessness of body and mind, with which most of us are more than familiar, experience has shown that a good way to begin practicing mindfulness is to bring the body to a standstill and just sit down. Our mind, of course, is another story.

The practitioner usually sits cross-legged on a cushion of some kind, which raises the buttocks off the floor and aligns the hips somewhat higher than the knees. This position supports good spinal alignment for an upright, relaxed, and stable sitting posture and creates an uplifted and dignified feeling for the practitioner. (Try sitting up straight with your knees higher than your hips and feel the strain this produces in your back.)

Let's return to our horse-and-rider analogy for a moment. Sooner or later the horse will tire out and stop for a rest. At that point, if you can gather yourself, you'll have the opportunity to remount the horse and take your seat properly in the saddle. According to the renowned Tibetan Buddhist meditation master Chögyam Trungpa Rinpoche, meditation or mindfulness practice could be described as learning to *hold your seat* properly, not only while seated on the cushion during formal meditation but even more importantly in the midst of your life.[6] In dressage training, it is common for the trainer to control the horse on a lunge line, guiding the horse in circles while the rider focuses on developing their dressage "sea legs"—a relaxed position in which the rider learns to let their pelvis and entire body move in unison with the horse. As you work on developing your seat and your communication with the horse, the trainer often calls out firmly, "Hold your seat, hold your seat."

In sitting meditation, we take our seat properly on the meditation cushion with good posture, mimicking the principles of dressage. Then, if we have committed to sit for thirty minutes, we *hold our seat* and remain on the cushion despite our mind generating a thousand reasons why we should get up or end our meditation early. Holding your seat also has to do with maintaining good physical posture on the cushion and with maintaining proper meditation technique. Just as the dressage rider is learning to move in unison with the energy of the horse, in mindfulness training you learn to ride the energy of the mind. The idea is not to manipulate the mind but rather to become one with it.

Sit on a meditation cushion or chair and find a posture that feels naturally uplifted and dignified, relaxed and sustainable. Begin by just noticing how you feel in the moment. If physical challenges prevent you from sitting, you can always try mindfulness meditation while standing or lying down. To minimize distractions, you may find it helpful to lower your eyes while keeping your head straight, resting your gaze in a relaxed manner four to six feet in front of you. If sitting, you can simply rest your hands, palms down, on your thighs slightly above your knees.

This practice session involves several steps, and I invite you to simply explore your present moment experience with openness and curiosity, welcoming whatever arises in your field of awareness. By allowing your experience to simply be as it is and not rejecting any aspect of it, you gradually let yourself come home—more and more, breath after breath. (Again, you could read through this instruction and then try it out, or listen to the audio recording available at SoundsTrue.com/store/rrpractices.)

Mindfulness of Body
Let's begin by bringing your attention to your body, just noticing how you feel. Pay attention to the contact between your palms and your thighs, between your seat or legs and the cushion or chair, between your legs or feet and the ground. Notice your breath flowing in and out and all the sensations that accompany each in-breath and out-breath.

With gentle curiosity, scan your body for feelings of comfort or discomfort, pleasure or pain, relaxation or tension, and everything in between, just noticing how it feels to be fully present in your body right now, moment to moment. As much as you can, dismiss any need for your body to be any other way than it is in this moment and accept whatever you are feeling without judgment. We have bodies. Bodies experience pleasure and pain, comfort and discomfort. That's what bodies do. Physical sensations are just the energy, the aliveness of the body. So the invitation is to simply sit and appreciate being alive in your body, including any discomfort, as best you can, with equanimity and ease.

Through the practice of mindfulness meditation, we have the opportunity to discover or reclaim our inherent dignity as human beings by rising above our habitual, fear-based comfort-seeking animal instincts and habits to embrace the entirety of our experience in the moment. We do not need to spend the rest of our lives living in fear (and sometimes terror) of discomfort and pain while chasing after comfort and pleasure like junkies or addicts.

Sit for a few minutes, just appreciating the miracle of life in your body, the arising and falling away of physical sensations of all kinds. If your attention wanders, gently bring it back to the sensations of your body and breathing as they come and go, arising and falling away continuously.

Mindfulness of Feeling (Emotion)

Now, if you would, bring your attention to your emotional body—to your heart, so to speak. With genuine interest and kindness, simply notice any moods, feelings, or emotional tones that may be present. Be curious about and willing to feel whatever arises moment to moment—feelings of contentment, sadness, anger, boredom, frustration, gladness, peace, joy, and so forth. We are emotional beings. We feel. We have emotional feeling and sensing pathways and centers in our brain. Some people say that we have an emotional dimension to our subtle energy body as well. Whatever we may be feeling in any given moment is completely okay, natural, and human—just part of our shared humanity. Of course, it matters quite a bit how or whether we act or react in relation to our emotional experiences, but there is no reason whatsoever to feel bad about any emotion we might be experiencing, even uncomfortable feelings such as envy, jealousy, or hatred.

Try sitting for a few minutes, appreciating these feelings as they ebb and flow, moment to moment. If your attention drifts, just gently bring it back again to your body and breath, and then turn it once more to whatever moods, feelings, or emotions are arising for you.

Mindfulness of Mind (Thoughts)

Next, without getting overly involved in them, just notice your thoughts as they come up, stick around for a while, and eventually fall away, one thought followed by another. We have minds, and minds produce thoughts. Our higher cognitive abilities, along with our capacity for feeling, are what make us human. There is nothing wrong with thinking. It is just the cognitive activity of the mind and neuronal activity of the brain. Try just watching the flow of thoughts, noticing the gaps in that flow with relaxed curiosity and interest. How does your mind feel? How does it appear to move?

Maybe you are having lots of thoughts, maybe just a few. Some thoughts may be about the past, others about the future. It's all good. Mindfulness meditation is not about suppressing or eliminating thoughts. Rather, it's about changing our relationship to thoughts. It's about becoming aware of thoughts rather than remaining lost in them. Over time, if we just let the thoughts be, the mind tends to quiet down all by itself. Again, we are responsible for what thoughts we do or do not act on, but there is no reason whatsoever to feel bad about any thought we might have, no matter how abhorrent or absurd it seems. Minds produce endless thoughts—it's just what they do.

Try sitting for a few minutes, grounded in awareness of your body and breath, just noticing and feeling your thoughts come and go of their own accord. If you space out or get lost in your thoughts, gently bring your attention back to your body and breath, noticing the flow of thoughts as they arise and fall away.

Innate Goodness and Worthiness

This is the last stage of this practice session. As best you can, bring your attention to the entirety of your experience—physical, emotional, and cognitive—noticing whatever arises in your awareness, moment to moment. See if you can relax the conditioned mind and its endless preferences for things it likes and its aversion for things it doesn't. Whatever comes up is just your present, very human experience, and there is nothing wrong with it or you. You are not broken. You don't need fixing. You have no reason to be embarrassed whatsoever. You are a human being with a basically good body, heart, and mind. And you are completely worthy to be alive and present right here, right now, breathing the air and sitting on the earth. This is your home, and you belong here.

For the next few minutes, relax any need or desire to be or feel any other way. Give yourself full permission to be just as you are. Feel your humanity, your innate worthiness, your unconditional basic goodness. If your attention wanders, gently bring it back to the felt experience of your body and breath and to this basic quality of being and feeling your innate worthiness, grounded in the experience of our shared humanity.

I recommend trying this practice for fifteen to twenty minutes. At different times you might choose to focus more on physical sensations or other sense perceptions, emotions, or the activity of your cognitive mind. You could also just do your best to experience whatever arises in your field of awareness during the session. When you finish, reflect on what happened. What did you notice? Please remember that it's not a matter of evaluating or critiquing your meditation or mindfulness practice. There really isn't such a thing as a good or bad meditation session, so try not to make a big deal about whatever comes up, no matter how sublime or painful. The point is to simply become increasingly familiar with the workings, rhythms, and patterns of your own mind, heart, and body.

Mindfulness is a way of befriending ourselves and our experience. **JON KABAT-ZINN**

FURTHER INSTRUCTIONS FOR MINDFULNESS PRACTICE

Working with Thoughts

You may notice that your mind produces lots of thoughts whenever you try a mindfulness practice such as the last exercise. In fact, you may become so distracted by the seemingly endless stream of thoughts that you find it difficult to stay with your experience at all. So what do you do about that? The answer is quite simple: nothing!

The classic instruction for working with thoughts in mindfulness meditation is to just let them be as they are, moment to moment. Like all the sense perceptions—tactile, visual, auditory, olfactory, and gustatory—thoughts come up, stick around for a while, and then fade away. With this flow in mind, we simply do our best to let it happen, trying to avoid suppressing or chasing thoughts as they come and go. And whenever we do notice that we have become involved in our thoughts—so much so that we are no longer present to the rest of our experience—we simply notice that and gently return to the immediate experience of aliveness in our body and all the sensations that make up the experience we call breathing.

It doesn't matter if our mind wanders hundreds or thousands of times. Each time it happens, we gently return our focus to our posture and breath, to the present moment. By doing this, we train our mind to awaken from the dream or trance of distractedness and learn to relax into our natural, innate wakefulness.

> We are willing to feel whatever arises without needing to hang on to it or push it away.

Working with Emotions

In mindfulness practice, we work with emotions just as we do with thoughts or any other sense perception, simply letting them be as they are, neither suppressing nor indulging them. When we do get caught up in challenging emotions such as fear, sadness, anger, and jealousy, the energy can completely overtake our mind, leading to anxiety and depression or agitation, hostility, and aggression. We can also become overly attached to positive emotional states, leading to elation and a lack of clarity. Either reaction is an obstacle to the mindfulness practice. The solution is to feel the emotion(s) as they are and simply regard any storylines accompanying the emotional state as bundles of thoughts, nothing more. By letting go of the storylines and feeling the raw energy of the emotion(s) directly, we can discover the natural wakefulness and wisdom within any emotional experience. For example, the energy of anger contains tremendous clarity; sadness connects us to our heart.

Basically, we work with thoughts and emotions in exactly the same way, welcoming them and letting them be as they are in each moment. We feel them and then let them go. In meditation, we call this *touch and go*. We touch our experience for just a moment and then we let it go. We are willing to feel whatever arises without needing to hang on to it or push it away. Clearly, this is easier to do with thoughts than with intense emotions. However challenging it may be, learning to hold your seat in the midst of emotional upheavals through mindfulness training offers a tangible doorway to freedom, peace, and happiness.

Witnessing Versus Sensing, Observing Versus Feeling

There are two different modes of mindfulness; both are helpful to cultivate. The first is witnessing or observing your moment-to-moment experience in the way described above. Witnessing is somewhat like sitting on a riverbank while watching the water flow by with all of its various ripples and eddies, branches and leaves. They're there for a moment and then they're gone, passing somewhere beyond your field of perception.

The second mode is direct sensing or feeling. Here, there is less of an obvious subject-object relationship and more simply being with or *in* the feeling, sensation, perception, or emotion. Returning to the river analogy, this mode is more like sliding off the riverbank into the water and feeling the water directly—the immediate coolness and wetness of the water itself. So if you're practicing mindfulness of breathing, you're not so much observing the sensation of breathing as you are becoming the breath or being the breath. I encourage you to explore both approaches and see what each offers you.

Neuroscience Note

These two modes of mindfulness actually use different neural pathways in the brain. Witnessing employs circuits along the midline of the brain (front to back) related to the sense of self. Direct sensing involves the lateral regions of the left and right hemispheres of the brain, which have more to do with the felt sense of embodiment. Both are important when it comes to developing our capacity for mindfulness and awareness.[7]

Emotional intelligence is the ability to perceive emotions,
to access and generate emotions so as to assist thought,
to understand emotions and emotional knowledge, and to
reflectively regulate emotions so as to promote emotional and
intellectual growth. **JOHN D. MAYER AND PETER SALOVEY**

3

THE POWER OF EMPATHIC AWARENESS

L et's face it—we're living in challenging times. Despite significant
scientific and technological progress, many of our institutions
appear all but incapable of dealing with our most pressing social,
economic, environmental, and political challenges. Widespread terrorism, ethnic cleansing, genocide, war, and refugee crises seem to
simply be the new normal, a global reality. Environmental degradation
and the extinction of living species continue at alarming rates; and we
can no longer deny the realities of human-caused climate change. The
divide between the superrich and the rest of us fuels political corrup-
tion and undermines democracy.

While advances in technology and self-employed jobs and careers
have created opportunities and mobility for many, these fortunate
people actually constitute an elite minority, globally privileged by their
access to higher education. Nuclear arms proliferation has expanded to
rogue states, and terrorist groups may be just steps away from getting
their hands on nuclear or chemical weapons of mass destruction. Here
in the United States, we seem more divided and polarized culturally

and politically than ever before. Overt racism and hate crimes appear to be on the rise. Gun violence in some major cities has reached epidemic proportions. We are in the midst of a national opioid epidemic, the worst drug abuse crisis in US history.

In the face of all this uncertainty, tragedy, and outright mess, it's more important than ever to be aware, resilient, and ready to respond to life's challenges as skillfully as we can. For this reason, the path of Radical Responsibility is all about living consciously and owning our choices and their impact. To do so, we need to cultivate awareness at every level of experience, especially when it comes to emotional awareness. To make good choices, we need accurate information about ourselves and others, and we also need to understand and appreciate how we respond to and feel about the challenges we face every day.

> During my fourteen years in prison, emotional awareness literally kept me alive.

During my fourteen years in prison, emotional awareness—the ability to track my own and others' emotional states—literally kept me alive. It also allowed me to accomplish a great deal of good in an extremely challenging environment. Today this same emotional awareness is foundational to my skills as a leader, teacher, consultant, and coach working in various arenas, including our criminal justice system, postconflict zones, and business enterprises. In this chapter I want to unpack what I mean by emotional awareness and emotional intelligence. In doing so, I will rely heavily on Daniel Goleman's four-quadrant model (depicted in figure 3.1), which provides an excellent framework for our Radical Responsibility journey of personal transformation while optimizing our day-to-day readiness to meet life's challenges with skill and relative equanimity.

WHAT IS EMOTIONAL INTELLIGENCE?

Most of us are probably familiar with IQ (intelligence quotient) as a measure of intelligence. A person's IQ is determined by scores on various tests that evaluate short-term memory, reasoning ability, and verbal recall. People can marginally improve test scores through practice or by lowering their test anxiety, but the measure is fairly static and, if anything, diminishes with age. In contrast, *emotional intelligence* (sometimes referenced as EQ but more commonly as EI) can be enhanced over time and perhaps throughout a person's life span. EI describes an array of intelligences that enable us to navigate the emotional, social, and political complexities of life with skill and grace.

The kind of intelligence measured by IQ tests can certainly help us excel and succeed in numerous endeavors. And we know that successful people in various fields do, in fact, typically have high IQ scores. Nonetheless, ultimate success in life—and certainly overall happiness—may have more to do with developing higher levels of emotional intelligence, regardless of our IQ. I'm sure we all know some truly smart people who are neither successful nor happy.

Daniel Goleman's 1995 bestseller *Emotional Intelligence: Why It Can Matter More Than IQ* launched this subject into the mainstream. Since then, EI has become one of the most intensively studied and widely promoted qualities of effective leadership.

Research has demonstrated that higher levels of EI clearly distinguish great leaders from ordinary ones and the general population.[1] As Goleman states, EI is the "sine qua non of leadership."[2] A high IQ might get you a job, but you need EI to actually thrive and succeed at that job. Research also demonstrates that IQ accounts for only about 20 percent of our overall success in life and that EI is a much more significant determinate of both personal and professional success.[3]

Okay, so here's the breakdown: Goleman's EI model originally included twenty-five competencies organized in five different clusters, but he later simplified the model (lucky for us) to the four quadrants depicted in figure 3.1. The most common terms used today for Goleman's four quadrants are: (1) *self-awareness*, (2) *self-management*, (3) *social awareness*, and (4) *relationship management*. In the quadrants shown here (adapted from Goleman and based on my own work), the two on top have to do with *recognition* and the two below are about *regulation*. The two quadrants on the left deal with *self*, whereas the two on the right with *other* (the social dimension).

I often refer to Radical Responsibility as training in *mindfulness-based emotional intelligence* (MBEI). I'm not going to cover EI with the depth that it deserves in this chapter, but this entire book is specifically designed to optimize your emotional intelligence in service of personal evolution and effectiveness. My purpose in this chapter is to lay out Goleman's map for you as a useful framework for better understanding our Radical Responsibility journey together.

SELF-AWARENESS

The self-awareness quadrant addresses the human psyche—the psychological, emotional, and spiritual dimensions of the self and their interconnectedness. Enhancing our self-awareness means getting to know how we function internally—basically, understanding what makes us tick. This includes developing greater awareness of our childhood and social conditioning; habitual patterns of thinking and behaving; fears; coping mechanisms and adaptive strategies; emotional triggers and hot buttons; underlying core beliefs, traumas, and internalized shame; shadow dynamics; and inherited biases and prejudices regarding nationality, race, gender, sexual orientation, socioeconomic class, and so on.

Increasing our capacity for self-awareness enhances moment-to-moment awareness of our emotional states and their relationship to our physiology and our underlying experiences of met and unmet or challenged needs—for example, love, connection, autonomy, respect, validation, security. Ultimately it involves transforming our internal landscape from one dominated by fear-based conditioning and internalized shame and unworthiness to one characterized by self-understanding, self-empathy, self-worth, and a greater capacity for self-agency. As we will explore in chapter 13, self-awareness also includes developing a relationship with the *heart-mind* (or *big mind*) and increasing our ability to rely on that vast and undefinable (yet realizable) dimension of our being.

4-Quadrants of Emotional Intelligence (EI)

Self-Awareness

- Emotional self-awareness
- Accurate self-assessment
- Emotional & needs literacy
- Self-worth/self-confidence

Social Awareness

- Empathy & caring
- Organizational awareness
- Service orientation

Self-Management

- Physiological self-regulation
- Emotion regulation & balance
- Integrity & trustworthiness
- Self-motivation & initiative

Relationship Management

- Communication skills
- Influence & inspiration
- Teamwork & collaboration
- Conflict management

FIGURE 3.1

Goleman's four-quadrant model of emotional intelligence (EI)

Here are some essential characteristics of emotional self-awareness:

- We recognize our feelings in the moment. We're emotionally *literate* in the sense that we can accurately identify different emotions and assess our current emotional state as it's happening.

- We can see the links between thoughts and emotions, and we understand the relationship between emotions and our perceptions of met or unmet needs.

- We are aware of our emotional triggers as well as our habitual patterns of reactivity and the storylines we use to justify them.

- We are familiar with how our emotional reactivity affects our performance and concerned with how it impacts others.

- We recognize that while emotions are a valid and important dimension of our human experience (and potentially sources of profound insight), they are also transitory in nature and often stem from misperceptions, assumptions, or limited interpretations of what is actually occurring in the present moment.

- We are able to feel our emotional experiences in the moment. We appreciate their richness and subtlety without hanging on to any particular feeling or indulging in reactive behaviors.

- We are aware of our inherited biases and prejudices. We do our best to set them aside in order to act with respect, inclusivity, cultural humility, and compassion.

SELF-MANAGEMENT

The good news is that increasing self-awareness naturally leads to greater capacity for self-management. What's more, we can learn specific skills for regulating our physiology, emotions, and behavior. (In fact, you did this in chapter 2 by enhancing your attention with mindfulness practices.) Our Radical Responsibility journey together will help you better understand and manage your own psychology, physiology, and neurobiology, positioning you to optimally *respond*—rather than *react*—to life's daily challenges with creativity, courage, compassion, and dignity.

A consistent daily mindfulness practice leads to more emotional balance.

Self-management skills allow you to exercise good judgment and make smart decisions even when distressed. Just to be clear, when I say *self-management*, I'm definitely not talking about ignoring or suppressing emotions. Rather, self-management allows you to feel your emotions and even appreciate their intelligence, all while maintaining the composure needed to avoid reactive behaviors that might prove problematic or harmful. In this way, you can make intelligent and beneficial decisions informed by emotional awareness.

We will explore lots of methods for self-regulation throughout this book, but one of the simplest (repeated by countless parents to their children over the years) is often attributed to Thomas Jefferson: "When angry, count to ten before you speak. If very angry, count to one hundred."[4] I'll go over the science behind this in chapter 7, but by the time we count to ten (or one hundred), we have probably released ourselves sufficiently from the grip of the fight-or-flight mechanism and regained enough access to the rational parts of our neocortex to respond more appropriately to whatever triggered us in the first place. And if we take a deep belly breath with each count, this *state-shifting* method will be even more effective in rebalancing our autonomic nervous system. In short, it enables us to downregulate our physiological and emotional state just enough to avoid impulsive reactivity and make better decisions for ourselves and others.

If you skipped or just skimmed the last chapter, here's a reason to go back: thousands of studies from current neuroscience—in addition to thousands of years of recorded human experience—clearly inform us that a consistent daily mindfulness practice leads to more emotional balance and an increased ability for emotion regulation, even in the heat of battle, so to speak. We generally feel more cognitively and emotionally balanced by the end of a meditation session. Of course, this isn't always the case, but it's a fact that most people feel more balanced on days when they practice than on days when they don't. But you'll never know until you try it out yourself.

Improving our capacity for self-management and emotion regulation has received ample attention in the business world recently. As most of us can attest, emotional reactivity can disrupt work teams and undermine organizational success in countless ways. Leaders who lack self-management skills often create fear-based, oppressive, and unsafe work environments for their employees. In my work as an organizational consultant, I have witnessed far too many senior managers wreak havoc on their companies due to their lack of self-regulation skills. In one case, a brilliant business owner, who vacillated between magnanimous and tyrannical management styles and was prone to emotional outbursts and bullying behaviors, drove his successful company to a complete collapse. Investors and longtime employees lost millions of dollars—in many cases, their life savings.

The SCARF model of brain-based leadership developed by David Rock, founder of the Neuroleadership Institute, is based on the recognition that employees and managers often react to the perception of unmet needs as if their very lives were at stake. The acronym SCARF stands for five basic human needs characteristic of business and organizational settings: status, certainty, autonomy, relatedness, and fairness.[5] Brain research shows that when people feel that these needs are threatened or unmet, they experience the same physiological and neurobiological reactions that occur when their lives are actually in danger.

It's no wonder then, that people behave in some business meetings as if the building were literally on fire! The next time you experience this type of reaction (from yourself or others), just remember that the brain and nervous system need an "all clear" message that everything is safe, in addition to the time and space it takes to rebalance. When it's you reacting, this might mean excusing yourself from the meeting to walk around the block and take some deep breaths. If you're witnessing a coworker's behavior, it might be helpful to convey safety with a reassuring tone of voice while skillfully suggesting a break that may be overdue anyway. From personal experience I can tell you that the last thing any of us needs when emotionally triggered is for someone else to challenge our perceptions or tell us to "calm down." Our brain will only interpret that as another threat.

Trainers and coaches employing the SCARF model help managers create working environments that minimize threats and maximize the rewards related to the basic needs for status, certainty, autonomy, relatedness, and fairness. They also coach individuals to manage their own reactivity and perceptions related to these needs. Learning to label a need when it feels threatened—for example, "This project is really challenging my autonomy and fairness needs"—rather than getting caught up in all the storylines around it can provide us with just enough cognitive and emotional distance to more rationally assess a situation. We can also question our perceptions and assumptions, and explore the possibility of seeing the dynamic in a new light, preferably in a way that feels less threatening. This skill is known as *cognitive reappraisal*. Labeling and reappraisal are both effective strategies to add to our self-regulation tool kit.

Self-management also allows us to maintain standards of integrity and congruency between our values and behaviors, even when we are under pressure. These qualities can easily become undermined when we allow our reptilian brain to take over. For example, in the heat of battle, we might find ourselves lying and giving into fear and survival instincts, even though we place a high value on personal honesty and integrity.

A healthy capacity for self-management also helps us keep the commitments we make to ourselves around things such as diet and exercise, or other disciplines for personal and spiritual development. Self-management skills allow us to be flexible and to handle ambiguity as well as multiple demands and changing priorities in our personal and professional lives. Our ability to build trust, to be reliable and genuine with others, to admit our own mistakes, and to take a principled stance even when it is unpopular are all functions of self-regulation.

Finally, our capacity for self-empowerment and intrinsic reward are also related to effective self-management skills. Being less reactive to external circumstances leads to a sense of internal agency, resilience, and confidence; it also lessens our dependency on validation and rewards from outside ourselves. We've likely all heard or used this classic excuse: "The devil made me do it." Well, the so-called devil is likely our reptilian brain, but blaming our bad behaviors on it won't get us far in life. Being an adult means taking responsibility for managing our reptilian brain's fight-or-flight mechanisms, no matter how loudly the alarm bells (amygdalae) are clanging in the limbic brain. (For more information on the physiology and brain science of emotional triggering, check out chapter 7.)

To review, here are some highly effective self-regulation tools to help you follow the Radical Responsibility path:

- Stick to a daily mindfulness practice (see chapter 2).

- Use breathing techniques to downregulate
  your nervous system (for example, the straw
  breathing practice you'll learn in chapter 7).

- Label triggered emotional states (anger, fear, frustration,
  etc.), and also identify and name the underlying needs you
  may be perceiving as unmet or threatened (see chapter 6).

- Look at things from a different perspective
  (cognitive reappraisal).

- Use a calm, clear voice even when dealing
  with distressing situations.

SOCIAL AWARENESS

You think your pain and your heartbreak are unprecedented in the history of the world, but then you read. It was books that taught me that the things that tormented me most were the very things that connected me with all the people who were alive, or who had ever been alive. **JAMES BALDWIN**

This quadrant in Goleman's EI model is focused on developing a number of competencies related to others: empathy and caring, organizational awareness, and having a service orientation.

Empathy and Caring: The Empathetic Heart-Mind

Social awareness and empathy both refer to our ability to feel what others are feeling—to sense what may be going on for them. It means we can tune in to others, respect their concerns, and care about their feelings. This ability involves listening well, paying attention to body language and vocal tone, and doing so out of genuine caring.

Of course, we can never know exactly what another person is feeling. However, as we get older and go through various hardships, most of us begin to recognize that others have experienced similar challenges. We begin to realize that a surprising number of our joys and sorrows are universal, and that knowledge empowers us to feel a stronger connection with and greater compassion for others. We become more interested in what they think and feel, as well as how they perceive the world. Our curiosity and openness to what's going on around us increases, especially when it comes to the people we live and work with every day. We may even begin to sense our interconnectedness with all human beings, and all forms of life, for that matter.

Empathy and compassion may be somewhat conflated in Goleman's model, as they often are in common usage. However, some researchers and clinicians define empathy more narrowly as our capacity to feel what others are feeling. For them, compassion refers specifically to concern for others and the motivation to help or relieve their pain. As it turns out, recent brain studies demonstrate that empathy and compassion involve different neural circuitry. Such studies also show that the experience of empathy can lead either to feelings of empathic concern and compassion or to empathic distress and aversive feelings. Taking the above distinction to heart, the burnout that happens when people are overexposed to human suffering (say, first responders and ER medical professionals) is actually *empathy fatigue*. *Compassion fatigue* is considered a misnomer, because compassion actually supports healthy psychological functioning.[6]

With this in mind, I suggest using the term *empathic heart-mind*. I'll talk about this a lot more in chapter 13, but for now I'll simply say that the empathic heart-mind is what allows us to have greater sensitivity regarding the feelings and needs of others in addition to the capacity to genuinely care about their well-being.

Organizational Awareness

We all live and work within various systems—family, social network, workplace, spiritual community, and so on—that operate at different orders of complexity. Goleman and others describe *organizational awareness* as a key competency for leaders within the social awareness quadrant. Whether we think of ourselves as leaders or not, we all clearly benefit from being able to understand these systems from top to bottom, inside out, and outside in.

Specifically, Goleman uses *organizational awareness* to refer to a higher order empathic awareness that includes the entire landscape of organizations and systems. To successfully navigate our way within a particular organization or system, we need to understand what the rules are, how decisions are made, how to influence such decisions, and how to effect change. We also need lots of insight into the culture, politics, and power dynamics of the landscape we're attempting to navigate. All of this requires a kind of holistic empathic awareness at the systems level.

Service Orientation

The final competency within the social awareness quadrant of Goleman's EI model is *service orientation*. Having a strong service orientation simply means that we are focused on providing service and valuable experiences to others.

Landing in federal prison with a thirty-year sentence for drug smuggling and a long history of alcohol and drug abuse, I fortunately realized I needed help and immediately joined the prison's 12-step recovery group. At my first meeting, an outside volunteer—John B., who would later become my sponsor and good friend—told the whole group, "If you really want this program to work for you, become someone who makes it available to others." My sponsor emphasized this basic message of step 12, the final step, to me again and again, and it stuck with me. So for fourteen years I served in every volunteer service position within the 12-step group and eventually sponsored fellow prisoners in the program, frequently facilitating a weekly 12-step book study in the education department where I worked as a GED/ESL instructor. Inspired by my first meditation teacher, who served humanity 24/7 his entire life, and the dedicated service and wise counsel of my 12-step sponsor, service to others became my primary life focus during my prison years (and since). This included starting the first hospice program inside a prison and spending most of my free time with fellow prisoners dying of AIDS, cancer, and other illnesses. I also led a twice-weekly meditation group in the prison chapel.

We can awaken from the trance of consumption by becoming creators instead of consumers.

I simply discovered living this way to be the best way to do my time and the most dignified and rewarding way to live my life. In the modern Western world, we are all trained from birth to be good, mindless consumers. Of course, we can't escape from being consumers all together, but from the perspective of Radical Responsibility, we can make every effort to consume consciously and wisely. By embracing the path of Radical Responsibility and a path of service to others, we can awaken from the trance of consumption by becoming creators instead of consumers, focusing on contribution and service to our communities, humanity, and life itself.

RELATIONSHIP MANAGEMENT

Just as developing greater self-awareness naturally increases our capacity for self-management, enhancing our social awareness means boosting our facility for skillful relationship management. Social awareness basically provides us with more (and better) data about the world and the people we relate with on a regular basis. This information quite naturally allows us to more skillfully interact with others.

Imagine for a moment that you are driving down the road in your car and suddenly the bright sun hits your dirty windshield. You suddenly find yourself all but blinded by the sun's glare and are barely able to see the road ahead. You feel anxious as you tighten your grip on the wheel and squint at the road ahead, hoping to avoid hitting another car. You want to pull off the road but can't even see well enough to do that safely.

> With relationship management, we consciously bring our best intentions and most emotionally intelligent, skillful, and wise self.

You spot a service station and manage to safely pull up to the pumps, get out of your car, and clean your windshield, doing a thorough job with a new sense of purpose. Eventually you pull back onto the road, and even with the bright sun you're able to see the road clearly. In fact, with your super-clean and transparent windshield, you can see way down the road. You relax your grip on the wheel and simply enjoy the drive, with just the right balance of alertness and relaxation. Why? Because you are getting all the information you need to see the road clearly and drive safely. In much the same way, enhancing your social awareness provides you with the data you need to navigate relationships with skill and confidence.

The term *relationship management* may be off-putting for some; it may imply some kind of manipulation. For this reason, I sometimes use the terms *effective relationship skills* or *skillful communication* for this quadrant. In the Radical Responsibility model, this is also the domain of *Authentic Relationship* (see chapter 11). However, when you consider how much drama and conflict arise from "unmanaged" relationships, perhaps the standard usage isn't so bad. *Management* in this sense merely means engaging in our relationships with kindness and skill.

With relationship management, we consciously bring our best intentions and most emotionally intelligent, skillful, and wise self to our daily interactions with others. Proficiently managing relationships for mutual benefit requires effective communication skills, the ability to influence and inspire others in positive ways, a team-oriented mindset, and the aptitude for navigating conflicts with ingenuity and grace. Sounds great, right?

There are lots of famous examples of leaders who embody all of this. One of my favorites is Nelson Mandela. Released in 1990 after twenty-seven years of imprisonment, Mandela worked with then president F. W. de Klerk to negotiate the end to apartheid and organize the first multiracial general election. This brought Mandela and his African National Congress party to power in 1994, gaining South Africa its first black African president. During his presidency, Mandela managed to skillfully guide his country through a remarkable transformation, focusing on ending institutionalized racism and racial injustice, promoting reconciliation between adversaries, and building a multiracial, multicultural democracy. Mandela's ability to navigate dangerous waters and guide his country through a seemingly impossible journey of healing and transformation required extraordinary levels of emotional intelligence.

MINDFULNESS-BASED EMOTIONAL INTELLIGENCE (MBEI)

Our approach to cultivating emotional intelligence begins with mindfulness. We use mindfulness to train a quality of attention that is strong both in clarity and stability. We then direct this power-charged attention to the physiological aspects of emotion so we can perceive emotion with high vividness and resolution. The ability to perceive the emotional experience at a high level of clarity and resolution builds the foundation for emotional intelligence. **CHADE-MENG TAN**

By now I hope it's clear that mindfulness is crucial to cultivating your emotional intelligence. If you haven't completed all the exercises and tried the mindfulness practices at least once, stop here and go back. Please don't shortchange yourself and rush ahead for the "good stuff," because it's all good stuff (especially the hands-on work). Please also keep in mind that my intention is to set you up for the long run—Radical Responsibility is a marathon, not a sprint.

The connection between mindfulness, a form of present-moment awareness, and self-awareness is clear. Mindfulness is also an effective aid to self-management, as it involves bringing our attention back to the object of mindfulness whenever our minds wander. Additionally, mindfulness of body and breath are both keys to regulating our own physiology and emotional states. Focused outwardly, mindfulness is the gateway to enhancing social awareness. Finally, mindfulness also boosts our capacity for skillful relationship management, including skills and practices I'll refer to as *mindful communication*, *mindful listening*, and *mindful speech*.

The Radical Responsibility model is in large part grounded in the context and skills of mindfulness-based emotional intelligence (MBEI). In fact, I envisioned this book as an MBEI manual for personal and social transformation. I have included these two chapters on mindfulness and emotional intelligence here early on for a reason—you'll need them both for the Radical Responsibility journey ahead.

PART II

THE CHALLENGE

How We Ended Up
Where We Are

The fact is that the human capacity for life in the world always implies an ability to transcend and to be alienated from the processes of life itself, while vitality and liveliness can be conserved only to the extent that men are willing to take the burden, the toil and trouble of life, upon themselves. **HANNAH ARENDT**

4

THE HUMAN CONDITION
a Fragile Beginning

Have you ever had one of those moments in which you realize that some aspect of your world has just imploded? And although you can sense that you are responsible for the catastrophe, you can't for the life of you understand what the heck happened? You look in the mirror and try to recognize the person you see staring back at you, attempting to comprehend what motivated you to do what you did. It just makes no sense to you.

We may have a vague sense that our actions are somehow engrained in us, carried over from our past, perhaps far back in our childhood. Still, we may not see a clear-cut path back to the precise moment in which a particular pattern took root. This lack of clarity is understandable—our personalities are formed through a complex combination of genetics, epigenetics (environmental influences on genetic expression), childhood experiences, and a lifetime of conditioning.

EARLY CHILDHOOD CONDITIONING

We are born very fragile beings, completely dependent on others for our survival. During the first six months of life, we do not possess a separate self-structure at all. Whenever we don't feel secure, held, or protected—basically anytime we feel pain, hunger, or fear—we cry out in distress. Our attachment to our parents or other caregivers is our only reference point, and for good reason.

Infants may show signs of budding independence around four months of age, but generally the process of individuation begins at six or seven months and runs throughout childhood, adolescence, and even into adulthood. The formation of a self-structure at the most rudimentary level is guided by our moment-to-moment experience of getting our basic needs met or not. Once we sense our separateness, there's no going back to the security of a unitary state with our primary caregiver, much less the safety of the womb.

If we grow up in a fairly stable, secure, and loving environment, the self-structure we develop is relatively functional but still oriented toward survival and, for this reason, essentially fear-based. If we are raised in a less-than-ideal environment with significant gaps in our care (or, in tragic cases, abuse and trauma), we are more likely to develop a less functional self-structure that is more prone to struggle and suffering. Even the most benevolent and conscientious parents cannot keep a young child comfortable and secure all the time, no matter how hard they try. Imagine a nine-month-old who suffers an earache. Under the best circumstances, it may take hours for the parents to acquire the necessary medication to treat the earache and for the medicine to take effect. What's going on for that child during that time frame? The parents are doing everything they can, but the child is still in extreme pain, which is likely a terrifying experience.

Every time a child experiences a gap in having their basic needs—food, warmth, affection, security, and so forth—satisfied, the process of self-formation becomes more tenuous and driven by fear. Over the early months and years of our life, we patch together the best self-structure we can out of whatever is available to us. When our early life is punctuated by the personal problems and problematic behaviors of caregivers, as mine was, that chaos becomes a familiar reference point for our existence. In a tragic way, it starts to feel like home. As adults, we can even find ourselves unconsciously attracted to similarly chaotic and painful situations.

Those of us who form healthy attachments to our parents during the first few years of life enter into this long process of self-formation with greater resilience and confidence. Those of us who experience less secure bonding (or for whom this bond was interrupted or broken) enter the journey more unsure of ourselves, struggling to navigate a sometimes terrifying world. Regardless of how stable our childhoods may have been, we all grow into adulthood with at least a mild sense of insecurity and existential anxiety. It's just the human condition. We all live to one degree or another with a shadow voice that tells us that we're not okay and not safe, no matter how skilled we have become at covering it up.

DEFINING MOMENTS

At some point in childhood, far too many of us experience harmful interactions with our caregivers or other adults. These experiences can take the form of neglect and abuse or simply some kind of shaming disapproval. Often these are moments when it becomes clear that our parents' love is not unconditional, that it can be withdrawn. Even mundane interactions can leave their marks, especially on children in the process of developing their psyches, and these events can rock our sense of emotional safety, belonging, and attachment. They can even threaten our sense of self to the core. During these defining moments, we learn to become small, to hide, or to disappear behind whatever mask of self-protection we can conjure.

EXERCISE   Defining Moments, Part 1

Please pick up your Radical Responsibility journal and write "Defining Moments" at the top of a page. Then just start writing whatever comes to mind from your childhood that might fit in this category.

Here's one of mine: I ran into the street after a ball. In doing so, I was almost hit by a car in front of our house, and my father freaked out and started screaming at me. Clearly it was a dumb thing to do, and my father was simply terrified that I could have been hit by that car. Nonetheless, I remember my whole being shrinking. I just wanted to disappear. I was flooded with shame and felt incredibly small—crushed, really.

I don't blame my father for his reaction. I can't imagine what it would have taken for him to handle that scare more gracefully; and as a result of his freak-out, I probably became less likely to run into the street without looking. Nonetheless, the experience also made a lasting negative impression on me.

Now it's your turn. What kind of memories come up for you? Write down as many as you can. When you're finished, take a moment to reflect on your experiences and think about the impact they made on how you are in the world.

SHAME

Shame is what we feel in reaction to rejection or the withdrawal of love. It's the emotion we experience when threatened with exclusion, when we get the message that we are unworthy, unwanted, or unlovable. Unfortunately, Western societies hold strongly to the belief that shaming is necessary in order to ensure acceptable behavior. This widely accepted notion of *positive shaming* serves as the basis of our modern punitive criminal justice system in the United States, leading to the current phenomena of mass incarceration and our broken and economically untenable criminal justice system.

Parents naturally want their children to be happy and safe. As part of that hope, many parents aspire for their kids to become successful members of their community, which means agreeing to all the norms, rules, and taboos that define membership in that community. Consciously or unconsciously, parents begin molding their children at an early age to fit in, not only by modeling appropriate behaviors but also by implying or stating threats of punishment, expulsion, or withdrawal of love. At the most basic level, a young child's acceptable behaviors elicit smiles or other signs of approval, while actions that trigger a parent's fears bring frowns, rejection, punishment, or other shaming behaviors. Just seeing embarrassment or fear in their parents' eyes is enough for a young child to internalize harmful messages of unworthiness.

Surrounded by these large, all-knowing, almost godlike figures, children react and adapt to their caregivers' behaviors as best they can with one prime directive: maintain their love and protection. For most of us, our message to our parents and the world becomes "Love me, don't leave me." In some cases, it might be "Love me, don't hit me." The adults in our lives are bound to act in ways that occasionally cause us to feel unsafe or even downright terrified. We adapt to these scary experiences as best we can, often twisting and contorting ourselves psychologically in order to assuage our terror. However, as children, we have limited cognitive and emotional resources to draw from in developing these coping strategies. We just do the best we can. In some cases, we instinctually react, doing what our young brains think will help us survive. In other cases, we may pick up adaptive strategies from older siblings or adults in our lives as we witness them interacting with each other. Whatever strategies we come up with become deeply imprinted in our young psyches, which means they show up later—for better or worse—in our adult personality and behaviors.

We often receive mixed messages during our most formative years. Some of us grew up with parents who were sometimes loving and supportive and at other times rejecting or even abusive. Parents might be excessively involved and invasive in some aspects of our lives and absent or neglectful in others. On top of this, caregivers convey social expectations—often quite rigidly—while regularly behaving otherwise. How is a young child supposed to make sense of all that?

Following these powerful early childhood influences, the onslaught of broader social conditioning begins as soon as we start watching television and going to school. The basic message from marketers, intent on training us to become active consumers, is that we are not enough and not okay as we are, but if we get our parents to buy their products, we might be happy, cool, or popular like the kids portrayed in the commercials or the kids at school who have the latest cool shoes or wear the right clothes. One can imagine how it is all but impossible for a young person, dealing with this barrage of conditioning and the pressure of fitting in, to have confidence in their authentic self and unconditional basic goodness.

Unless we are fortunate enough to attend a Montessori or other alternative school, the shame-based enculturation continues with our education from preschool onward. Most public and private schools have always embraced the reward-and-punishment approach to enculturating and educating kids. Recently, schools have become more and more focused on control and intimidation, even criminalizing nonconforming behaviors. They are using police and arrests to control young children in elementary school, creating what sociologists call the "school-to-prison pipeline," describing how disadvantaged kids especially are further marginalized and funneled into the criminal justice system.

All this confusing fear- and shame-based conditioning imprints very deeply in our psyches and neurobiology during our earliest, most formative years, because the younger we are, the more plastic or fluid our neural structures. As adults, we find ourselves carried along, mostly unconsciously, by this early childhood conditioning underlying our attitudes, thoughts, feelings, and behaviors. Our neural structures are less plastic as we get older, but change, even profound change, is nonetheless completely possibly, even at the neurobiological level. We will explore the phenomenon of *neuroplasticity* and brain-based strategies for change and transformation in chapters 7 and 8.

TRAUMA—OUR COLLECTIVE INHERITANCE

Trauma is the experience of any physical or emotional threat that overwhelms our coping mechanisms. It leaves imprints in our nervous system, especially when our fight-or-flight response is thwarted and we are unable to escape the traumatic circumstances. Multigenerational trauma can occur when survivors of war, genocide, racism, extreme poverty, and extreme oppression pass their experiences on to their children through various forms of neglect or abuse, begetting patterns in families that continue until broken or rerouted. Additionally, the field of epigenetics informs us that genes and their expression are influenced by our environment, altering the genes we passed on to our children. Such multigenerational trauma can result in post-traumatic stress disorder (PTSD) or related symptoms of anxiety, depression, addictive-compulsive behaviors, suicidality, and even abusive and violent behaviors. These negative impacts of trauma passed on from one generation to the next undermine resilience and leave individuals and their communities in a debilitated state, caught in dysfunctional cycles of addiction, abuse, poverty, unemployability, mental illness, and institutionalization.

Even though the roots of your family's issues may not be as grave as those described above, the multigenerational transfer of psychological challenges and toxicity impacts us all to one degree or another. We have all absorbed trauma from our family lineage.

No matter where you were born, East or West, your parents, grandparents, or great-grandparents, even as civilians, were likely impacted by World War II and other wars before or since. Generation after generation, families continue to be affected by the trauma of war, genocide, and refugee crises, resulting in alcoholism, substance abuse, mental illness, childhood neglect, and various forms of physical, emotional, and sexual abuse. Native Americans and African Americans in the United States—as well as indigenous people the world over—still suffer from the historical and multigenerational trauma inflicted upon their families by colonialism, genocide, and slavery. To one degree or another, those of us of European descent have likely internalized the guilt and shame of our ancestors' participation in the displacement and genocide of native peoples.

> Any experience of unconditional love we receive from our caregivers has a huge impact on how we develop as children and live as adults.

I'm not just trying to paint a dark picture of humanity here. Although we face substantial challenges ahead—especially concerning the environment—we are incredibly resilient as a species. Harvard psychologist Steven Pinker, in his highly acclaimed book *The Better Angels of Our Nature*, cites evidence of a declining rate of violent deaths from homicide, war, genocide, and terrorism, which is certainly hopeful news.[1] Nonetheless, we can't ignore the impact of several thousands of years of brutal and bloody conquest, war, and genocide.

The sum total of all the internalized trauma, shame, and accumulated toxicity resulting from the legacy of violence and oppression described above, along with every imaginable form of unskillful parenting, neglect, and abuse—to say nothing of unresolved oedipal issues and the collateral damage of sibling rivalries—presents no small psychological challenge to each new human being trying to navigate their way into functional adulthood in an ever more complex and crowded world.

POSITIVE PSYCHOLOGICAL IMPRINTS

Okay, time for some good news. Our childhood conditioning is not all negative. None of us had perfect childhoods, and usually it's a mixed bag of sorts. Fortunately, the positive experiences we have in early childhood also imprint deeply and become powerful drivers of our adult experience and behavior. For example, any experience of unconditional love we receive from our caregivers has a huge impact on how we develop as children and live as adults. The more unconditional love we receive, the more functional and loving we are as adults. We are social beings and need others to survive. Our ability to sustain healthy intimate, familial, social, and professional relationships has a lot to do with our ability to be empathic with others, a capacity directly related to the amount of love and empathy we received during our formative years.

I want to be clear—the purpose of this exercise is not to blame your parents. For the most part, they were just passing on what they received and did the best they could, given their own conditioning and whatever degree of self-awareness or psychological insight they possessed. The point here is to identify the type of input and modeling that informed your conditioning for the purpose of better understanding yourself. And while it's true that the degree to which you received unconditional love, empathy, and support during childhood influences your default capacity to be empathic and supportive with yourself and others now, the tools in this book will allow you to significantly enhance this capacity.

LIMITING CORE BELIEFS

Based on our inherited family and cultural legacy of conditioning, we form what are called *limiting core beliefs*. These are typically fear-based ideas about ourselves and the world around us, which mostly operate on a subconscious level and yet drive our moment-to-moment attitudes, perceptions, feelings, and behaviors. As children, we unquestioningly adopt many of the beliefs, attitudes, and emotional patterning of our parents or caregivers, older siblings, teachers, and others. Gradually we form a foundational worldview that impacts our entire life. We also develop core beliefs based on our interpretations and conclusions about the meaning of the behaviors of those around us, especially the influential adults and authority figures in our childhood.

In the early developmental stages of childhood, we typically see and interpret things in a very self-referenced manner, and we often assume that we are to blame for uncomfortable and painful situations where our physical, emotional, and social needs are not met. It is common, for example, for young children with divorcing parents to assume that the divorce is their fault and then carry associated negative feelings and beliefs about themselves into adulthood. We tend to put the worst spin on our challenging experiences, thereby forming fear-based—and ultimately self-limiting—conclusions about ourselves and the world.

> **Seeing clearly helps you break free from habitual patterns and make conscious, informed choices.**

Limiting core beliefs tend to shut down possibility and creativity. They also foster survival-based mindsets that focus on perceived scarcity and threats of all kinds, such as the world is a dangerous, scary place, and there's not enough love, food, money, fame, and the like, to go around. Additionally, most of us carry some deeply held ideas about how we ourselves are not enough—not attractive enough, not smart enough, not talented enough . . . you fill in the blank.

Here's a list of commonly held limiting core beliefs:

- I'm not good enough.

- I don't matter.

- I'm not lovable.

- I don't deserve anything.

- I'll never get a break.

- I'll just mess it up.

- I'm too lazy.

- There's something wrong with me.

- I might get hurt or hurt somebody.

- I'll never get ahead.

- Life is just too hard.

Do any of these sound familiar? Most of us will likely be able to recognize at least a couple of these statements in our recurring self-talk—that discursive and reactive conversation that goes on silently between our ears most of the time. Remember, limiting core beliefs usually operate outside of our awareness, but they influence our attitudes, thoughts, feelings, and behaviors. A good way to become familiar with them is simply to pay close attention to our self-talk.

◀)) **EXERCISE** Listening to Your Self-Talk to Discover Limiting Core Beliefs

Immediately after waking up in the morning, before doing anything else, allow yourself a moment of self-reflection. Set a strong intention to listen closely to your self-talk during the day. Set up several check-in times—for example, during meals or other break times—using your watch or cell phone alarm to remind you. Keep your Radical Responsibility journal nearby and write down any self-talk statements that express negative limiting core beliefs. At the end of the day, take some time to reflect on what you wrote down. Keep up this practice until you are able to clearly articulate the kind of underlying limiting core beliefs that dominate your self-talk.

Hopefully you are beginning to experience directly how we have been programmed for better or worse by our childhood experiences. Seeing and owning the extent to which negative childhood experiences and conditioning impacts your life can be a tough pill to swallow. Fortunately, recognizing these limiting core beliefs is the first step to freedom. Armed with this awareness, you can begin to transform these self-limiting beliefs or at least prevent them from unconsciously running your life. Seeing clearly helps you break free from habitual patterns and make conscious, informed choices that are more aligned with your authentic self and more likely to meet your long-term needs.

WHERE DO WE GO FROM HERE?

The human condition unexamined condemns us, to one degree or another, to a life driven by fear- and shame-based conditioning. This same human condition bravely examined, however, becomes the basis for the highest possibilities of human evolution. On the path of Radical Responsibility, you are invited to fearlessly investigate and see clearly the ways in which your own deeply ingrained beliefs and attitudes developed. The purpose of this investigation is not to place blame on others or develop excuses for yourself, but rather to access the insight, self-empathy, and self-understanding that will set you free. Doing so will enable you to transform in the direction of your own choosing and evolve toward your highest potential. At the very least, you'll finally understand what drives your behaviors today and shed some light on why you react to particular difficulties and relationship challenges the way you do.

Your complaints, your drama, your victim mentality, your whining, your blaming, and all of your excuses have never gotten you even a single step closer to your goals or dreams. Let go of your nonsense. Let go of the delusion that you deserve better and go earn it! Today is a new day! **STEVE MARABOLI**

5

STUCK ON THE DRAMA TRIANGLE AGAIN

Have you ever been called a drama queen (or drama king), or have you ever labeled someone else that way? The truth is that we all have an inner drama king or queen. As human beings, we're fascinated with drama, sometimes even addicted to it. Drama is the very essence and fuel of great literature, theater, and film. What would *Law and Order*, *The Wire*, or *Breaking Bad* be without drama? Since ancient times, three principal characters or roles have been at the core of nearly every form of theatrical drama—the hero, the villain, and the victim.

The next two chapters owe a lot to the groundbreaking work of Stephen Karpman and what he calls the Drama Triangle, a dysfunctional dynamic perpetuating negative and destructive drama. Karpman depicted this dynamic with these three roles: villain (persecutor), hero (rescuer), and the victim positioned at the corners of an equilateral triangle (see figure 5.1).[1] Though Karpman was awarded the Eric Berne Memorial Scientific Award for his work, I think he deserves the Nobel Prize in psychology for describing the heart of human conflict and suffering with such clarity.

Countless people have found Karpman's Drama Triangle to be one of the most liberating psychological distinctions ever identified. Understanding the toxic dynamics of triangulation and learning how to get off the Drama Triangle and avoid it wherever possible are foundational to the path of Radical Responsibility. By clearly seeing and owning our patterns of conditioned reactivity, we can finally move in the direction of genuine autonomy and self-empowerment.

We first learn the art of triangulation in our family of origin.

Some of you may be old enough to remember "Dudley Do-Right of the Mounties," a segment on *The Adventures of Rocky and Bullwinkle and Friends* that parodied early twentieth-century melodrama and a type of silent film known as "northerns" (similar to westerns, but with a northerly setting, usually Canada). Dudley Do-Right was a hapless but well-intentioned Canadian Mountie pitted against his archenemy, Snidely Whiplash, an archetypal villain dressed in black, complete with a top hat and well-oiled handlebar mustache. Dudley Do-Right—the bright-red-uniformed Mountie with (of course) blond hair, blue eyes, and white horse—is endlessly infatuated with Nell Fenwick, a classic damsel in distress also usually depicted with blonde hair and blue eyes. He is continually trying to save Nell from Snidely, the evil banker trying to take the orphaned Nell's home away from her. So here we have the classic melodrama with the hero (rescuer) in Dudley Do-Right, the villain (persecutor) as Snidely Whiplash, and the damsel in distress (victim), Nell Fenwick. The triangulation of these pivotal personas plays out in an entertaining fashion episode after episode. While today's dramatic films and televised programs may present more nuanced characters, they typically follow the same age-old script and unfortunately continue to perpetuate similar stereotypes.

Karpman's Drama Triangle demonstrates how the triangulation of these three personas, mindsets, or psychological positions (that is, persecutor, victim, and rescuer) creates endless human conflict and relational dysfunctionality. The interplay of these roles might be entertaining to watch on television, but the toxic conflict perpetuated by

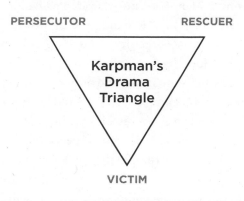

PERSECUTOR   RESCUER

Karpman's
Drama
Triangle

VICTIM

FIGURE 5.1

Stephen Karpman's Drama Triangle, adapted with permission

the Drama Triangle in actual life destroys families and wreaks havoc on communities and even entire societies.

What's the origin of this destructive dynamic? It's basically grounded in the human condition, which when unexamined and unchallenged leads to a fear- and survival-based approach to life, where we continually divide people into friends and enemies. We first learn the art of triangulation in our family of origin: Mom, Dad, and me (or any similar configuration of primary caregivers we may have had). When we don't get our needs met from one parent, we naturally approach the other and, if necessary, skillfully play one against the other until we get what we want or need. Unless our parents are unusually sophisticated and skilled at thwarting such efforts, we are likely successful, becoming master triangulators at an early age.

I want to be clear here that when talking about Karpman's Drama Triangle and the three positions of victim, persecutor, and rescuer, we are not labeling or calling people victims, persecutors, and rescuers. Rather, we are talking about survival-based psychological positions or mindsets we assume in a fear-based effort to meet our needs, regain a sense of control, and avoid feelings of uncertainty, vulnerability, and powerlessness.

Here's a funny and not-so-funny example that may feel familiar to a lot of us: Little Joey is whiling away his afterschool time playing in the backyard. George, Joey's father, gets home from work and discovers that Joey has completed neither chores nor homework. George calls his son inside and immediately starts berating him: "Joey, when are you going to grow up and be responsible? Once again you haven't done your chores or your homework. If you keep on this path, you're going to turn out to be a useless bum! Do you know that?" Hearing this lecture, Helen, Joey's mom, steps in to the rescue: "George, please don't talk to Joey like that. You're going to destroy his self-esteem. If Joey ends up a bum, it will be your fault for yelling at him all the time." Then Joey, who of course doesn't like being yelled at but nonetheless idolizes his father, turns to his mom and says, "Mom, don't yell at Dad. No wonder he's always yelling at me. It's because you're always picking on him." George, barely able to contain himself, then jumps on Joey again, "Joey, don't you dare talk back to your mother like that!"

As you can see, once the Drama Triangle is formed, it starts spinning of its own accord, building more and more toxic momentum, with the players moving from one position to another. In this case, Joey started in the victim position but moved on to rescue Dad and persecute Mom. George began in the persecutor role but moved on to rescue Mom and then returned to persecuting Joey, most likely with an internal stop on the victim position along the way. Helen started out in the rescuer position and then moved on to persecuting George. I'm sure we can all see how this particular Drama Triangle could perpetuate itself endlessly.

Of course, this example uses stereotypical gender roles. It could have just as easily involved a working mom and stay-at-home dad, two working parents, a gay couple, or a single parent with an absent other as the unacknowledged third player in the triangle. Whatever your own family structure or dynamics may have been growing up—or however they may be now for those of you with children at home—I imagine something like this particular drama sounds only too familiar. We could also imagine other scenarios that endlessly play out between couples, within families, or among coworkers and their bosses at work. Let's take a look at some of the dramas you are likely familiar with in your own life.

EXERCISE Familiar Dramas

Get out your Radical Responsibility journal and begin writing down some of the dramas that crop up repeatedly in your personal and work lives. Give your dramas catchy titles such as "The Taking-Out-the-Trash Drama," "Who-Left-the-Dirty-Dishes-in-the-Sink Drama," or "Why-Does-the-Boss-Play-Favorites Drama." After you've decided on the title, name who starts off in the victim, persecutor, and rescuer roles. Record as many of your dramas as you can. You can also include dramas you witness among your family, friends, and coworkers. The idea is to begin to see how pervasive this destructive dynamic really is and strengthen your motivation to avoid creating or participating in negative dramas. Like most of the exercises in this book, this is one worth coming back to and reflecting on repeatedly. Doing so will increase your insight into the nature of toxic drama and inspire you to live a happier life less impacted by this destructive dynamic.

Okay, before exploring further how the potentially dangerous and damaging toxicity of the Drama Triangle plays out in our lives and the world around us, let's take a deeper look at each of these three personas or psychological positions named by Karpman.

THE VICTIM PERSONA

To begin with, it's important to acknowledge that people are victimized. We know that terrible, horrible, heinous things happen to both adults and children. When someone is seriously victimized, they most likely need validation and support. Ideally that support empowers them to direct the trajectory of their own recovery and healing, receive the validation and/or justice needed or called for, and ultimately move beyond a sense of victimization and powerlessness to survivorship.

I led trainings for genocide survivors in Rwanda in 2010 and 2011, teaching the participants to work as para-trauma counselors at the grassroots, village level throughout the country. These trainings employed many of the skills, distinctions, and practices you are learning here on the Radical Responsibility path, integrated with training in the transformative justice and peace circle models. These amazing survivors of the horrific 1994 Rwandan genocide found the Drama Triangle and other Radical Responsibility distinctions (that we will explore in later chapters) to be incredibly helpful and empowering.

While the path of Radical Responsibility can clearly be helpful even in such extreme cases of mass violence and victimization, what we are exploring in this chapter has more to do with the ways we ourselves tend to feel victimized just because it's raining outside, or we can't afford to pay our cable bill, or someone broke a date with us, or our boss passed us over for a plum assignment. Most of us frequently find ourselves in the victim mindset in one way or the other. It occurs whenever we're unhappy with the way our life is going, and we believe that the cause of our unhappiness lives somewhere outside of ourselves. Additionally, we think that we are powerless to alter how we are feeling until the external circumstances change. Feeling stuck and helpless in this way, we often indulge in "poor me" thoughts and behaviors. We complain, orient ourselves mostly toward the problem (as opposed to solutions), and typically feel anxious, hurt, afraid, angry, hopeless, or depressed. In some cases, we may even use the victim position to get attention or play the victim card to gain power or control.

> We think that we are powerless to alter how we are feeling until the external circumstances change.

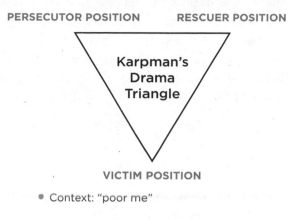

PERSECUTOR POSITION   **RESCUER POSITION**

Karpman's
Drama
Triangle

VICTIM POSITION

- Context: "poor me"

- Actions: complaining, blaming, attention seeking, tantrum throwing, manipulating

- Orientation: problems, complaints

- Mode: reactive, blaming

- Feelings: helpless, powerless, anxious, afraid, hurt, angry, hopeless, depressed

FIGURE 5.2 The victim position

EXERCISE My Victim Stories

Grab your Radical Responsibility journal and write "My Victim Stories" at the top of a page. Write down as many of your "poor me" stories as you can. Again, give them catchy titles such as "My Wife Doesn't Appreciate How Hard I Work," "My Kids Never Call Unless They Want Something," "My Boss Takes Credit for All My Great Ideas," and so on. Just keep writing for as long as you can. Come back to your list several times, see if you can discover even more of these stories, and reflect on what they do for you. What kind of results do you get when you play out these stories? How do they make you feel? How do you tend to act when you're under their spell?

A standard ritual in prison for getting to know your fellow prisoners is sharing or trading victim stories. It didn't take long for me to tire of the ritual (especially my own story), and I soon began to make every effort to avoid it. Is there any place in your life—at work or in other social settings—in which you engage in a similar ritual?

THE PERSECUTOR PERSONA

The persecutor mindset criticizes, judges, blames, belittles, negates, and tries to control or dominate others. The mode is reactive and attacking. Caught in the persecutor persona, we may feel afraid, irritated, angry, superior, self-righteous, or defensive. Typically we seek control and power in this way because, deep down, we feel insecure, uncertain, powerless, and defenseless. But what position on the Drama Triangle does that sound like? That's right—underlying the persecutor is the deeper psychological position of the victim. People who are chronic persecutors and abusers have almost certainly been persecuted and victimized in the past, usually as children. It's a sad truth that hurt people frequently hurt others. Fortunately, not all of us who have experienced some form of childhood maltreatment become chronic persecutors or abusers.

EXERCISE   My Persecutor Stories

Okay, now write "My Persecutor Stories" at the top of a page in your Radical Responsibility journal. List all your persecuting behaviors you can think of. What are some of the ways you "should" yourself and others? What brings out your criticism and judgment? How have you sought to control or dominate others? How have you engaged in passive-aggressive behaviors (making fun of people, picking on them, pushing their buttons, and so on)? Just keep writing until you have identified as many of these behaviors as you can. *(cont.)*

PERSECUTOR POSITION

- Context: "I'm right"

- Actions: criticizing, judging, blaming, controlling, dominating, attacking, abusing

- Orientation: problems, complaints

- Mode: reactive, attacking

- Feelings: anxious, fearful, angry, superior, righteous, defensive

- Underlying position: victim

RESCUER POSITION

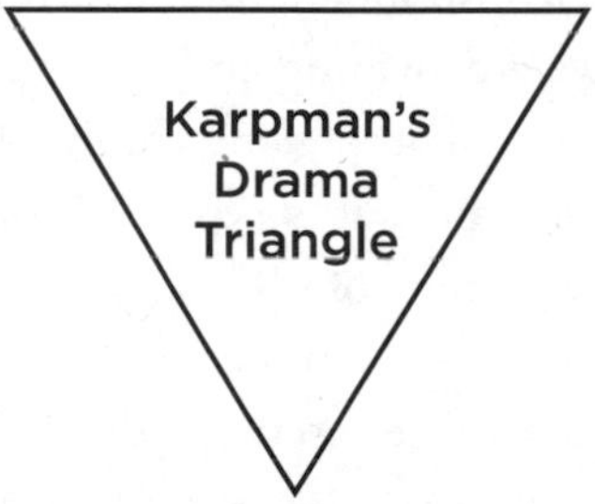

Karpman's
Drama
Triangle

VICTIM POSITION

- Context: "poor me"

- Actions: complaining, blaming, attention seeking, tantrum throwing, manipulating

- Orientation: problems, complaints

- Mode: reactive, blaming

- Feelings: helpless, powerless, anxious, afraid, hurt, angry, hopeless, depressed

FIGURE 5.3 The victim and persecutor positions

This may be a very uncomfortable reflective exercise, so don't forget to breathe. And try not to persecute yourself in the process. Again, this practice isn't about assigning blame but rather gaining some clarity and freedom from behaviors and attitudes that no longer serve you. We all inhabit these roles from time to time—it's just part of the human condition. However, we can also take steps to ensure that these personas don't continue to drive our destiny.

THE RESCUER PERSONA

This pole on the Drama Triangle represents the savior, fixer, or martyr archetype. We are not talking about rescuers in the traditional sense here—that is, *not* first responders, doctors, nurses, or people who jump in a river to save a drowning child—or anyone who works to help others out of genuine compassion. In this usage, the rescuer is a specific persona we take on that is typically related to someone else who is embodying the victim role. The rescuer is continually on the lookout for victims because the rescuer needs to be needed. And to the extent that we need to be rescuers, we need other people to be victims. Furthermore, in assuming the rescuer position, we enable others to take on or remain in the victim role.

The rescuer is oriented toward fixing other people and their problems, or acts like a kind of savior who goes around saving people from themselves. Rescuers give advice and assume authority or responsibility over others, and in the process enable and disempower their victims. Feeling states associated with the rescuer position may include smugness, superiority, self-righteousness, heroic, unappreciated, and overwhelm. Once again, underlying all of this is a sense of insecurity and powerlessness. Once more, the underlying psychological dynamic of the rescuer is the victim position.

Of course, people help others for all kinds of reasons. They may empathize with someone going through a hardship or be motivated by love, compassion, or a deep-seated desire to right an injustice in the world. None of us are *pure* rescuers. At the same time, few of us who regularly help and support others are completely free of the rescuer persona. When our natural instinct to support others is conflated with the rescuer dynamic—that is, our egoic need to feel needed or be the expert with the solutions—we aren't actually all that helpful. In fact, our "helping" often ends up enabling and/or disempowering others and encouraging them to resent us in the long run. If you are one of those people who everyone comes to with their problems, it may be that you are a good listener, but it could also have something to do with the rescuer persona. Recognizing that we sometimes get caught in the rescuer position is not about judging ourselves, and it's certainly no reason to stop helping others or abandon our career as a helping professional. It is simply about seeing these patterns clearly, so we can let go of the rescuer mindset as much as possible and learn to support others in a more empowering manner with a genuinely altruistic motivation.

I frequently train those in the helping professions (nurses, physicians, social workers, therapists, chaplains, and volunteers) in self-care strategies for cultivating greater wellness and resiliency. Caregivers are at risk for what we call *pathological altruism*, a form of rescuing behavior that leads to overwhelm and burnout. This has also been called *idiot compassion*, meaning compassion that's devoid of wisdom and discernment (in other words, rescuing).

> When our natural instinct to support others is conflated with the rescuer dynamic, we aren't actually all that helpful.

I also do a lot of training with volunteers who facilitate mindfulness programs for prisoners. Prison volunteers are naturally inspired to volunteer out of some kind of compassion or concern about the plight of those who are incarcerated. Though society may think of prisoners as persecutors who have caused harm to victims, volunteers tend to see prisoners as victims of racism, oppression, social neglect, and so on. Additionally, volunteers often project the persona of persecutor onto the correctional officers and other prison officials they deal with. To the extent that this occurs, volunteers place themselves in the rescuer position and are complicit in perpetuating

Drama Triangles. That's why I encourage volunteers to do their best to see everyone involved, prisoners and staff alike, as human beings just like the rest of us, struggling to meet their needs as best they can.

It goes without saying that far too many prisoners have, in fact, been victimized their entire lives, and there are certainly grave injustices that occur in our criminal justice system, especially in terms of race and socioeconomic status. At the same time, it's also true that many prisoners have committed harmful actions; in some cases, they have horribly violated and victimized others. Correctional officers and prison staff can unwittingly (or quite consciously) assume the role of persecutors, but a good number of them are doing their best to perform a tough and dangerous job while working to keep everyone safe. Their biggest concern may simply be getting home to their families in one piece at the end of each shift.

Finally, prison volunteers who unconsciously assume the rescuer persona are in danger of enabling or reinforcing a victim mindset in the prisoners with whom they work, which is highly counterproductive to the process of healing, rehabilitation, and transformation they aspire to facilitate. At the same time, projecting the persecutor persona onto the prison staff can undermine the effectiveness of their relationship with these professionals on whom they depend for access and their own safety.

EXERCISE   My Rescuer Stories

Okay, you know the drill by now. Pick up your Radical Responsibility journal, make a "My Rescuer Stories" heading, and start a list of ways you engage in rescuing (yourself and others)—trying to fix people, giving them unsolicited advice, seeing others (or yourself) as broken or helpless, feeling unappreciated by those we try so hard to help or save, and so on. Notice any habitual rescuing thoughts that come up too—for example, "This place would fall apart if it wasn't for me" or "If I don't go into work, nothing will get done." With compassion and clarity, just keep writing until you get a clear picture of your various styles and patterns of getting caught in the rescuer mindset.

PERSECUTOR POSITION

- Context: "I'm right"

- Actions: criticizing, judging, blaming, controlling, dominating, attacking, abusing

- Orientation: problems, complaints

- Mode: reactive, attacking

- Feelings: anxious, fearful, angry, superior, righteous, defensive

- Underlying position: victim

RESCUER POSITION

- Context: "I know"

- Actions: rescuing, saving, fixing, enabling, colluding, disempowering

- Orientation: problems & fixes, savior-martyr

- Mode: reactive, fixing

- Feelings: smug, superior, self-righteous, heroic, unappreciated, overwhelmed

- Underlying position: victim

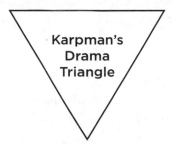

Karpman's Drama Triangle

VICTIM POSITION

- Context: "poor me"

- Actions: complaining, blaming, attention seeking, tantrum throwing, manipulating

- Orientation: problems, complaints

- Mode: reactive, blaming

- Feelings: helpless, powerless, anxious, afraid, hurt, angry, hopeless, depressed

FIGURE 5.4 The victim, persecutor, and rescuer positions

SPINNING DRAMA TRIANGLES

The three positions on the Drama Triangle embody fear-based strategies for obtaining or regaining a sense of power and control. These can be normal and reasonable human needs when they find healthy expression. But attempting to meet these needs with the unhealthy Drama Triangle strategies embodied in the victim, persecutor, and rescuer roles just fuels toxic drama, conflict, chaos, and suffering. We'll explore healthier expressions of personal power in chapter 12, where I'll present what I call the Empowerment Triangle.

As we saw in the example involving little Joey and his parents, once the Drama Triangle forms, it tends to spin, with players shifting positions continually, creating a toxic vortex of conflict, fear, and pain. I want to look at a few more related examples and then invite you to explore some of your own triangles. One thing to keep in mind: there are usually different versions of any given Drama Triangle, depending on the perspective of the players.

DIFFERENT PERSPECTIVES

Here's an example that might be only too familiar. Let's say you are driving to work, minding your own business, when suddenly you see the dreaded flashing lights of a police car in your rearview mirror. "Damn," you say, "I'm getting pulled over." As you pull to the side of the road, you are quite likely feeling victimized by the patrol officer. "I was barely speeding," you say to yourself. "Why aren't they chasing the real criminals?" As you wait for the officer to approach, you may even be thinking, "Oh, no . . . now my car insurance will go through the roof. This is going to cost me thousands of dollars. It's not fair." Clearly you are feeling victimized, and you have projected the persecutor role onto the police officer. If you have a fellow passenger, you may be soliciting their sympathy, inviting them to commiserate with you, to rescue you emotionally. You might even be thinking about a lawyer you know who could help you beat this thing in court.

While this particular version of the Drama Triangle may seem quite clear and compelling to you at the time, what do you think the police officer's perspective might be? In all likelihood, they see themselves not as a persecutor but as a rescuer. And who are they rescuing? Potential victims of your speeding, because to the officer, *you* are the persecutor or perpetrator. In this way, there are almost always competing versions of any Drama Triangle, one overlaying the other, which further increases the likelihood of conflict. As the players move from one role to another, desperately seeking an advantage, the triangle spins faster and faster, creating a nearly inescapable black hole of drama.

A DESTRUCTIVE FORCE

The toxic energy of unchecked Drama Triangles destroys individual lives and families, causing untold harm to children the world over. The destructive chaos perpetuated through the dynamic of these three roles can cause lasting wounds on entire communities, playing out on the world stage in the form of violent conflicts, wars, genocide, and the threat of nuclear annihilation. According to historian Matthew White, a staggering 203 million people were killed as a result of war and oppression in the twentieth century alone.[2] Of course, war and its horrors have been with us for a long, long time. We often think of it as a terrible fact of life that we are powerless to do anything about. Perhaps. But there is certainly one thing we can do something about: our own involvement with destructive dynamics of drama in our personal and work lives.

> With sufficient awareness and motivation, we can make different choices.

Hopefully I have made a compelling case regarding the dangers and potential destructivity of the Drama Triangle, especially when we allow these dramas to spin out of control, unchecked, all the while disowning our own role in creating and perpetuating them. The danger of getting caught up in the destructive dynamics of toxic triangulation may be inevitable, given the fear and survival tendencies of the human condition, but with sufficient awareness and motivation, we can make different choices. In the next chapter, we will explore how to recognize and get ourselves unhooked from the Drama Triangle.

PART III

TAKING CHARGE

Becoming the Captain
of Your Own Ship

6

GETTING OFF THE DRAMA TRIANGLE

Getting unhooked from whatever dramas you have created, landed in, been sucked into, or simply stumbled upon will profoundly change your life for the better. Countless participants in my trainings around the world have let me know that learning about the Drama Triangle has radically changed their lives (and those of their families) for the better. There are several interrelated pieces to the Radical Responsibility path, but this chapter outlines one of the most important ones. Here are six steps that will get you unhooked from just about any Drama Triangle you create or stumble into:

1. Recognize that you are on a Drama Triangle.

2. Stop. Don't act when triggered.

3. Take space and shift your state.

4. Own your feelings.

5. Identify your needs and communicate them clearly (when appropriate).

6. Make a boundary when necessary.

STEP 1 RECOGNIZE THAT YOU ARE ON A DRAMA TRIANGLE

Recognizing that you are on a Drama Triangle is probably the most difficult step of all. Most of the time, we don't recognize the Drama Triangle for what it is. We become entangled in the story and feel completely justified in whatever we think, feel, say, and do. We blame the situation and our feelings on others and disown our own role in creating or perpetuating the drama.

This is where your mindfulness practice plays a key role. Being mindful of your body allows you to recognize the physiological signs of drama activation; being mindful of your feelings helps you detect your emotional reactions; and being mindful of mind enables you to recognize the thought patterns that get kicked up by the drama. By learning to recognize all of these signs with mindfulness, you can release yourself from the grip of projection and blame and simply acknowledge that you're caught in a Drama Triangle, regardless of who instigated it.

It helps to make a conscious commitment to not act when triggered.

The victim position on the Drama Triangle is probably the easiest to recognize. Simply put, we feel victimized. That comes with its own brand of upset emotions (hurt, anxiety, anger, and so forth), physical sensations (shallow breathing, constricted chest, sweaty palms, tension in the neck and shoulders), and thoughts (captivating stories of powerlessness, injustice, and so on).

By contrast, the persecutor and rescuer roles don't always come with such telltale warning signs. However, these positions still manifest in our language, tone of voice, posture, and actions toward others, and they are also accompanied by particular thought patterns and sometimes subtle (but nonetheless recognizable) emotional states. We each have our particular style of acting out each of the three roles or personas on the Drama Triangle, so it's important to get to know all of your modes in order to recognize these habituated reactive states and behaviors on the spot.

EXERCISE   Drama Warnings

Under the heading "Drama Warnings" in your Radical Responsibility journal, write down all of the physiological, emotional, and mental signs you can think of that indicate to you that you're on—or are about to be on—a Drama Triangle. List as many as you can think of from each position; as I mentioned above, the victim mode might be the most obvious one. Please remember to practice self-compassion while you do this, and remember that this isn't about assigning blame to anyone, including yourself. These exercises are critical to your path of Radical Responsibility, as it is this degree of self-awareness and insight into your own psychology that will begin to set you free.

STEP 2   STOP. DON'T ACT WHEN TRIGGERED

Whenever you are able to recognize yourself getting hooked on the Drama Triangle, the next step is to stop and simply resist the urge to continue playing out your given role. If you are triggered—that is, you experience strong emotions and a heightened physiological state—your primary job is to self-regulate and not make the situation any worse. Until you're able to do this, you'll be under the spell of one of your old childhood tapes—the kind that projects a previous experience of feeling threatened or unsafe onto the landscape of the present. These stories generate emotional and neurobiological responses that convince us of the truth of our victimization, justify our persecution of others, or urge us into rescuing behaviors while further reinforcing these habitual patterns and neurobiological imprints.

For this reason, it is critical to recognize the drama for what it is and refuse to act until you're able to release yourself sufficiently from its grip. That can be a tall order, so it helps to make a conscious commitment to not act when triggered. I strongly encourage you to make some kind of vow that you can rely on when under duress, much like a marriage vow or any other important life commitment. It might help to write that statement down in your Radical Responsibility journal and even come up with some kind of meaningful ritual for taking the vow.

EXERCISE The Vow

Feel free to reword this in any way that works for you. For now, let's simply repeat this empowering statement three times (the magic number):

1. I will not act when triggered.

2. I will not act when triggered.

3. I will not act when triggered.

Then write the same vow at least three times (if not more) on a notable page in your Radical Responsibility journal. Remember to revisit your vow from time to time or reword it to keep the inspiration fresh.

STEP 3   TAKE SPACE AND SHIFT YOUR STATE

Before doing anything else, you need to address any kind of heightened or upregulated physiological and emotional state you're experiencing. So the next step is to *state shift*—to consciously release yourself from the grip of the fight-or-flight response and regain access to the rational decision-making capacity of your brain's *executive function*. (More details on this in the next chapter.)

Remember the adage about counting to ten when angry? There are all sorts of self-regulation techniques like this to help you shift your state. For some of us, going out for a walk by ourselves, listening to soothing music, or reading our favorite book can be extremely helpful strategies. For others, putting on some upbeat music and dancing works. Try different state-shifting techniques and notice which ones best change your physiology and mood. Learning to do this type of thing when emotionally triggered is critical to becoming the captain of your own ship and navigating the sometimes treacherous waters of human interactions with steadiness, wisdom, and grace.

EXERCISE   Counting to Ten

Think of a recent time when you felt emotionally triggered—the more triggered, the better. Bring this situation back to mind, reliving it as intensely and vividly as you can until you recognize the clear signs of being triggered—shallow breathing, accelerated heartbeat, anxiety, sadness, anger, racing thoughts, fearful thoughts, and so on. Whenever you can feel it clearly, just stop and begin counting to ten. With each progressive number, take a deep belly breath and notice how long it takes you to become untriggered and return to a more balanced physiological, emotional, and mental state. It doesn't matter how long it takes for this to happen—just keep breathing deeply and counting to ten again and again until you feel balanced and in control or in a responsive rather than reactive state.

STEP 4   OWN YOUR FEELINGS

This is one of the most critical junctures in your path off the Drama Triangle. Owning your feelings means to intentionally shift from blaming, projective language—*you* statements—to using empowering, reflective *I* statements. For example, instead of "You always do this to me—how dare you!" you communicate with a sense of ownership: "I'm feeling angry and confused right now." Engaging in blaming thoughts and language is like pouring gasoline on the fire of conflict and drama. On the other hand, the reflective process of identifying and owning your feelings helps you exit the Drama Triangle more quickly and further downregulates your physiology. I'll talk more about the science behind this in chapter 7, but for now I'll just add that engaging in the reflective process of recognizing and owning your feelings automatically shifts you from the survival-focused and reactive reptilian brain to the more rational and responsive functions of the neocortex.

Anger is an emotion commonly connected to drama and conflict. Some would argue that anger isn't really a primary emotion but rather a secondary one that masks feelings of fear, sadness, or hurt—emotions that leave us feeling perhaps more vulnerable. In this sense, it may instinctually be safer to feel and express anger. For this reason, when we identify anger in ourselves and own that feeling with the internal statement "I'm angry," we may want to reflect further and try on "I'm sad," "I'm afraid," or "I'm hurt" to see if those feelings are also present.

In the process of identifying and owning your feelings—especially strong emotions such as anger—you can sometimes get hooked back into the Drama Triangle with thoughts that assign blame for your feelings on others (for example, "Yes, I'm angry, but she *made* me angry"). Try not to get sidetracked in this way. It's actually possible to recognize that while your emotions may in some way be tied to external events or the actions of others, they are nonetheless your feelings, regardless of their origin. You may further recognize that these feelings are quite familiar and perhaps at least as much related to past experiences as present circumstances. Most importantly, the shift from *you* statements to *I* statements, from projection and blaming language to reflection and ownership language, provides an immediate exit from the Drama Triangle by shifting us from an unconsciously and/or habitually reactive mode to a conscious reflective and potentially responsive mode.

EXERCISE   Own Your Feelings

Create an "Own Your Feelings" headline on a new page in your Radical Responsibility journal. Write down as many short blaming statements related to feeling states that you can think of, or note the ones you remember thinking or saying when triggered. Here are a few examples:

- How dare you!

- You're pissing me off!

- Stop making me miserable!

- Fuck you!

- You started this!

Get into it and have fun! Once you have filled up a page or two, go back and look at each statement in turn. What would the correlated *I* statement be? (For example, "How dare you!" might be "I feel shocked and confused.") Write those *I* statements down next to each blaming sentence or phrase. When finished, reflect on any insights that may have come up and write those down as well.

STEP 5   IDENTIFY YOUR NEEDS AND COMMUNICATE THEM CLEARLY (WHEN APPROPRIATE)

In order to work with step 5, we need to understand the source of our feelings and the relationship between feelings and needs. Even if we don't want to admit it, most of us are fairly convinced that our feelings are caused by external circumstances or the actions of others. There seems to be an immediate connection between feelings and external events, as if the two were glued together: My boss overlooks me and I feel hurt; my kids leave a mess and I feel angry; my friend breaks a date and I feel sad and rejected.

These stories seem so true, but let's unpack them and dig a little deeper. First of all, what do we mean by *needs*? Well, we all certainly have needs such as food, warmth, and shelter. That's a given. But what other universal needs do we all share? Here's a short list I came up with:

- love

- respect

- trusting relationships

- autonomy

- self-worth

- creative expression

- security

- meaningful work

- a sense of purpose

- a connection to something greater than self

EXERCISE   Your List of Universal Needs

What would your list look like? Feel free to use your Radical Responsibility journal for this one. You might come up with something a lot different from my list, but I'll bet we share at least some of the same needs. Furthermore, if we looked at each other's lists side by side, I bet we'd recognize something that we'd like to add to our own. Even if we prioritize our needs differently, as humans there are universal requirements in life that we nonetheless share.

When we perceive our needs as being met, we feel happy, content, at ease, grateful, appreciative, and so on. When we perceive that our needs aren't met, watch out—fear, anxiety, hurt, anger, jealousy, and all sorts of challenging feelings come up. Notice how I use the word *perceive* in relation to my experience of met or unmet needs. With a little honest reflection, I think we can all admit that our perceptions are at best limited and incomplete interpretations of what is actually going on in the moment. We can probably also acknowledge that our perceptions are sometimes *misperceptions*—we occasionally miss the mark entirely or imagine something unreal all together. As it turns out, our perceptions—accurate or otherwise—determine our experience. If we remember this fact, it will help decrease the power of the mistaken belief that external events and people are the primary cause of our internal experience. We will be more likely to look within and examine and own our perceptions and feelings.

> We can all admit that our perceptions are at best limited and incomplete interpretations of what is actually going on.

Another clue is the very observable fact that different people react very differently to the same circumstances. Let's take the case of an employee layoff, for example. The way one feels and reacts will likely have a lot to do with one's circumstances. A single parent living from paycheck to paycheck with kids at home to care for may naturally feel quite upset and anxious, even desperate; on the other hand, someone with abundant savings and fewer dependents may feel considerably more laid-back about the layoff or even see it as a welcome change opening up new possibilities. Nonetheless, even when people's circumstances surrounding a given event are largely similar, you'll still find a lot of diversity in how each person perceives and responds to that event, given the differences in our childhood conditioning, personalities, and emotional resilience.

Our perceptions are not purely objective assessments of reality. We notice the things that have importance to us, assign them meaning and preference, and tend to ignore (or actually not perceive) stimuli in the environment that don't seem to pertain to our lives. As human beings, we are meaning-making machines—we constantly add meaning to everything we perceive, externally and internally, through our senses. We hear a sound outside and the narrative starts: "Oh, that must be Mr. McGillicutty out there mowing his lawn. But why is he doing it so early on a Saturday morning while I'm trying to sleep?" Or maybe our boss walks by our desk at work and doesn't stop to say hello: "Well, that's rude. Why is she upset at me? Is it because I didn't get that report in on time yesterday? Oh no, there goes that raise I was hoping for. She's never liked me much anyway . . ."

Has this type of thing ever happened to you? How about when the same boss walks by later in the day and beams a warm smile in your direction, inquiring about your plans for the weekend? Feeling tremendously relieved, you might say, "Wow, I really misread you earlier today. You walked right by my desk, without saying a word. I thought you were upset with me about something." Your boss says, "What? No, you're doing a great job. Oh, you mean this morning? I was just distracted—difficult phone call with a supplier, nothing to do with you!"

Our perceptions are not purely objective assessments of reality.

In this case, all's well that ends well. However, for much of the day you were stewing in a brew of your own making, experiencing all kinds of uncomfortable and challenging feelings you assumed were caused by the actions of another person. In fact, your perceptions were way off and the entire experience was self-generated. These realizations can be a little embarrassing and humbling when they happen to you (at least they are when they happen to me), but the point here is to realize just how loaded with assumptions or false impressions our perceptions can be much of the time. Remembering that makes it a lot more difficult to blame our feelings on others or things outside of ourselves. And because our internal landscape is largely under our control, we can always check out our perceptions and underlying assumptions with others. Doing so, we may find that our needs are not actually threatened after all.

When we stop blaming other people for our feelings and refrain from demanding that others meet a particular need of ours (say, approval), we might actually be able to communicate our needs to them in a less charged way and make the meeting of that particular need more likely. To that point, it's critically important to share our needs simply as *information*. In other words, our needs are not *demands*. If we can arrive at the understanding that no one person or situation is capable of meeting all (or any, in some cases) of our needs, then we won't feel the need to make demands on others. And when we learn to straightforwardly communicate our needs as information—free of charged or demanding energy—people are much more likely to respond in positive and mutually beneficial ways.

STEP 6   MAKE A BOUNDARY WHEN NECESSARY

Sometimes our best efforts to tactfully or peacefully extricate ourselves from the Drama Triangle may not be enough. Sometimes we need to make a boundary and communicate it as clearly as we can to others—for example, "This conversation appears to be headed in a not-so-helpful direction; let's revisit this some other time when we've had a chance to cool down and reflect a bit," or "If you don't leave immediately, I will call the police." Boundaries are fairly simple in principle: they're all about knowing when to say yes and when to say no, both to ourselves and others. If I can't say yes to myself, I'll miss out on a lot of joy and fun. On the other hand, if I can't say no to myself, if I can't delay immediate gratification to pursue more important goals, I won't be able to accomplish much in life. Likewise, if I can't say yes to others, it will be difficult to create or sustain meaningful relationships, and if I can't say no to them, I'll end up overcommitted, overwhelmed, burned out, and probably resentful.

We all know people who have poor boundaries. Typically their lives are full of chaos, drama, and a lot of relational pain. If we're really honest with ourselves, we might see places or times in our own lives in which our own boundaries could use some work. Boundary issues are fairly common. Perhaps one or both of our parents or other caregivers failed to model good boundaries, or maybe they were overly invasive or too protective, making it difficult for us to establish a clear sense of self. Having some insight as to the source of our boundary issues may be helpful—especially if the dynamic is still playing out with our parents—but it doesn't actually help all that much to blame our parents or anyone else for our condition. As adults on the path of Radical Responsibility, the most important thing is to focus on developing good boundaries now.

Just practice saying yes and no to yourself and others until you become good at it—until it becomes natural. The better boundaries you have, the less likely you'll end up on the Drama Triangle; and when you occasionally get caught on one, the less likely you'll get stuck there. Boundaries generate a type of presence and protective energy. When you have clear boundaries, people sense it, and anyone looking to create drama will typically steer clear of you and go elsewhere in search of more willing Drama Triangle playmates.

During my years in prison, there were potentially dangerous dramas waiting around every corner. A lack of mindfulness and awareness would get me into trouble quickly. By observing the environment and the interaction of my fellow prisoners carefully, I learned that carrying myself too passively or timidly would attract predators but walking around too aggressively or belligerently would attract challengers. Following the classic middle way approach from the Buddhist tradition, I learned to carry myself confidently yet humbly and respectfully. By having very clear boundaries and mindfully paying attention to the world around me, I managed to avoid 99 percent of the daily drama and insanity of prison life. Sadly, that was not the case for many of my fellow prisoners.

EXERCISE   Boundaries (Good and Poor)

Open your Radical Responsibility journal and write "Good Boundaries" at the top of one page and "Poor Boundaries" at the top of another. Under the first heading, write down areas where you generally have good boundaries or are willing to make boundaries in your personal and professional lives. Once you've done that, under the second heading, write down examples of situations where you have poor boundaries or aren't willing to make boundaries in your personal and professional lives. Now go back and reflect on both pages. What benefits do you get from setting and keeping healthy boundaries? What price do you pay for not doing so?

Please remember that this is not about beating yourself up or feeling bad about yourself. It's just another opportunity to see clearly and understand how your conditioning—in this case, your boundaries or lack thereof—impacts your freedom, personal effectiveness, and the quality of your relationships. As always, the first step to making desired adjustments in your life is to see where you are currently with clarity and compassion.

AVOIDING THE DRAMA TRIANGLE OUTRIGHT

Okay, now that you've learned the steps to free yourself from the toxicity and suffering of the Drama Triangle, you're well on your way to discovering a newfound personal freedom. But wouldn't it be great to also know how to stay away from drama in the first place? Before we move on to other aspects of Radical Responsibility, let's explore some strategies for avoiding the Drama Triangle outright.

> Become as familiar as you can with your drama hooks and all the ways in which they disguise themselves.

Recognize Your Drama Hooks

The beloved teacher Pema Chödrön, an American-born nun in the Tibetan Buddhist tradition, has written several popular books, including the audiobook *Don't Bite the Hook: Finding Freedom from Anger, Resentment, and Other Destructive Emotions.* Chödrön uses the word *hook* to translate the Tibetan term *shenpa*, which is typically translated as "attachment."[1] It can also refer to the emotional charge we feel in relation to certain situations or people in which we get mentally and emotionally snagged, as if by something sharp and barbed like a fish hook. Once hooked, it can be hard to get away.

We all live in a sea of floating drama hooks. Some have your name on them, some are meant for your spouse or partner, and some are just for me. When one of your drama hooks passes by, I might not even notice it, because it doesn't correlate with my issues, interests, stories, or habits. But when one of mine floats by, watch out. Here it comes with a juicy chunk of bait on it. I begin salivating, my palms sweat, and my heart races. At that moment I'm ready to swallow it whole, but what I really need to do is recognize it for what it actually is—a one-way ticket for another spin on the dreaded Drama Triangle. If I can see that, then I have a better chance of avoiding being hooked.

What we need to do at that moment is take a few deep breaths and just hold on, hold our seat (remember chapter 2) for ten seconds, maybe thirty seconds tops. That's often enough to avoid biting (or worse, swallowing) the hook. Of course, even with the best intentions, we all get hooked now and then. When that happens, don't beat yourself up; understand that it happens to the best of us. Go right back to the steps for getting off the Drama Triangle and gently take the hook out of your mouth.

It really helps to become as familiar as you can with your drama hooks and all the ways in which they disguise themselves. Most of us have quite a few, but we can learn to recognize them and get better at feeling their approach, which in itself is an excellent practice of mindfulness and awareness. Finally, in addition to all of the tips above for getting off and staying off the Drama Triangle, here are some concluding suggestions that will help you remain drama free (as much as possible):

- Avoid gossiping and rescuing behaviors.

- Try not to take things so personally (in other words, don't bite the hook).

- Don't rely on assumptions about others' intentions. Ask questions and find out what's really going on.

- Make clear agreements with others and keep them. When you can't, proactively renegotiate.

- Don't sweat the small stuff. Save your energy for the tough challenges that will certainly come your way.

Every man can, if he so desires, become the sculptor
of his own brain. **SANTIAGO RAMÓN Y CAJAL**

7

TAKING CHARGE OF YOUR DESTINY

Brain Science 101

want to shift gears a little and explore some of the basics of physiology and brain science in order to clarify the way we are wired for
survival, the nature of emotional triggering, and the stress response.
I also want to look at what mind-body medicine pioneer Herbert
Benson calls the *relaxation response*[1] and give you some skills for practicing self-regulation (the second quadrant in Goleman's model of
emotional intelligence). Learning how to self-regulate better empowers us to have greater emotional resilience and more confidence in our
ability to handle life's challenges. The path of Radical Responsibility
involves taking ownership of our thoughts, feelings, and behaviors, in
addition to the circumstances we face day in and day out; and doing so
requires both resilience and the capacity to regulate our own physiology and emotions. Learning to self-regulate in this way gives us access
to the optimal responsive state of mind where we can exercise choice,
even in the most difficult of circumstances.

THE THREE-POUND UNIVERSE

The brain weighs about three pounds and has a consistency similar to tofu. It has 1.1 trillion cells—considerably more cells than stars in the Milky Way (estimated at somewhere between 100 and 400 billion). Signals cross our brain through neural networks in a tenth of a second, and a typical neuron makes 5,000 connections with other neurons, establishing a network of 500 trillion synapses—a system more complex than almost anything we can conceive of. The brain is always on. It operates 24 hours per day, 7 days a week, 365 days per year fueled by glucose and oxygen. Like a data bank, it stores things. Some of these things entertain us, some comfort us, some bore us, and others torture us. To employ a common metaphor, our habitual thoughts and behaviors create a road map in the brain—a system of frequently traversed highways and byways that become very much like well-worn physiological pathways or even ruts. The popular expression "I'm stuck in a rut" says it all.

TRIUNE BRAIN THEORY

Although out of favor with many scientists working today, Paul MacLean's *triune brain theory* is an intuitively sensible model for understanding more about our brain and its relationship to our behaviors. MacLean, a physician and neuroscientist, theorized that the brain has three basic structures related to our evolutionary development: a reptilian complex, a paleomammalian midbrain structure, and the neomammalian neocortex.[2] Per MacLean, the reptilian brain includes the brain stem and the basal ganglia. It's primarily involved with instinctual survival behaviors such as aggression, dominance, territoriality, and ritual displays. By contrast, the paleomammalian brain, or midbrain, is described as being composed of the limbic system, which includes the septum, amygdala, hippocampus, and cingulate cortex. It is mostly concerned with emotional processing, the motivations that drive feeding and reproductive behaviors, maternal and parental instincts, relational bonding, and the emotional component involved in making decisions. Finally, the neomammalian brain in MacLean's model includes the cerebral neocortex, which is responsible for higher cognitive functions such as abstract thought, planning, reasoning, and decision-making, as well as our capacity for complex social interactions.

For the purposes of this book (and the Radical Responsibility path in general), I use the terms *reptilian*, *limbic*, and *neocortex* as a kind of shorthand to refer to these three functional areas of the brain. All of these activities described above involve complex, integrated interactions within the whole system of the brain, so please understand this somewhat oversimplified breakdown described in MacLean's model for what it is—a helpful rubric of sorts. That being said:

- The reptilian complex (the *survival* brain) regulates hormones and supervises fear-based avoidance behaviors intended to promote survival.

- The limbic system (the *feeling* brain) processes emotions; generates behaviors to meet our needs for food, warmth, shelter, and procreation; and informs our decision-making process with emotional intelligence.

- The neocortex (the *thinking* brain) plans, reasons, makes most decisions, and manages social interactions.

There are two more concepts in common use today that will be important for our exploration of brain science as it applies to Radical Responsibility: *executive function* and *amygdala hijack*.

EXECUTIVE FUNCTION

The executive function, located primarily within the neocortex, or thinking brain, plays a critical organizing role in the brain, operating much like a CEO making overall decisions about resource allocation within an organization. The executive function decides where to place our mental and physical resources, how to organize and prioritize brain activity, and where to direct our attention in each moment, as well as the degree of focus. Specifically, executive function refers to a set of cognitive processes necessary for:

- planning

- correcting errors

- trouble-shooting

- problem-solving

- moral reasoning

- effective decision-making

- resisting strong habitual tendencies

- controlling cognitive processes in order to achieve desired outcomes (for example, attention control, reappraisal, and working memory)

These processes primarily involve neural structures in the prefrontal regions of the brain's frontal lobes (the dorsolateral prefrontal cortex, the anterior cingulate cortex, and the orbital frontal cortex), but they also involve connections to other areas of the neocortex in addition to the basal ganglia and the brain stem. However, for the sake of simplicity, I'll generally refer to executive function as residing in the neocortex.

When we are emotionally triggered we generally don't make the best decisions.

AMYGDALA HIJACK

Coined by Daniel Goleman, amygdala hijack refers to a sudden emotional flooding that is disproportionate to the actual stimulus.[3] In other words, it imputes a much greater perceived emotional or physical threat based on past memories. The amygdalae are emotional processing centers, part of the limbic system in the midbrain (paleomammalian brain), that function like warning systems. They alert the reptilian brain to activate the HPA (hypothalamus-pituitary-adrenal) axis, ultimately releasing cortisol into the bloodstream and triggering the fight-flight-freeze response to perceived threats. To put it more simply, the feeling brain *hijacks* the thinking brain, causing emotional flooding and reactivity disproportionate to whatever is actually occurring in the moment. And when our locus of control shifts to the fight-flight-freeze response (under the control of the reptilian brain), we have less access to our executive function and our ability to make rational, objective, or wise decisions.

EXERCISE   Emotional Triggers

Reflect for a moment on times when you have been emotionally triggered and then done or said something really dumb (or at least not so smart) that landed you in some kind of mess. If you are like most of us, several examples will come to mind. Grab your Radical Responsibility journal and under the heading "Emotional Triggers" write down the most striking examples that come to mind. After doing so, reflect on the situations you described. Note the actual emotional triggers that were activated—abandonment, jealousy, overwhelm, shame, and so on.

Okay, now pick one of the examples you wrote down and do your best to revisit it. Close your eyes and bring that experience into the present moment, as if it were happening right now. Do the best you can to allow yourself to feel the emotional trigger again. What physiological, emotional, and mental signs of stress can you note as the trigger begins to take hold? Or thinking back to when this event actually happened, what were some of the signs of activation you can remember?

Now take a few deep breaths and relax into gentle belly breathing, counting each breath (if that's helpful) and allowing the trigger or memories of the incident to subside. Notice any changes in your physiological, emotional, and mental state as you begin to calm down and become more balanced. Reflect on what you are learning about the signs of stress response and your ability to modify that response.

As we all know only too well from personal experience, when we are emotionally triggered we generally don't make the best decisions. Remember the state-shifting practice of counting to ten? What happens by the time we count to ten? In lay terms, we start to chill out. That helps us regain access to the executive function in our neocortex and our ability to make good decisions. Counting is a higher order cognitive process that requires use of our neocortex; it's just something that the reptilian brain can't do. (How many lizards do you know that can count?) Counting distracts us from the emotionally triggering stimulus and forces us to bring the neocortex back online, allowing us to engage our executive function and make more rational decisions.

Amygdala hijack can also refer to the rush of positive emotions such as sudden, uproarious laughter in response to a funny joke, or intense joy brought on by a sense of heartfelt connection. So if you find yourself fortunate enough to experience some kind of ecstasy, enjoy it! But wait until you come back down to earth before making any major life decisions (such as getting married or giving all your money away, for example).

FIGHT, FLIGHT, OR FREEZE

Once, as a child, some friends and I were enjoying an ill-advised game of throwing snowballs at passing cars. Suddenly, one of the vehicles screeched to a halt. The driver and his passenger jumped out and started chasing us. The older kids ran away, but I dove into some nearby bushes to hide. Fear overtook me, and I physically froze—my entire body shut down and became utterly immobile. Luckily the men didn't see me; they took off after the other kids. Even so, I was frozen in place, and to this day I clearly remember that feeling of visceral paralysis—the only time I've experienced it in my life. Working with people who have experienced significant trauma, I regularly hear accounts of people having similar experiences of intense shutdown.

Even if you haven't experienced shutting down to this degree, most of us are quite familiar with the momentary freeze that can occur in response to sudden fear or alarm. These types of involuntary pauses give our brain time to assess the situation before moving into either fight, flight, or freeze mode. You're probably familiar with the stress response that occurs whenever our brain accurately or inaccurately perceives potential danger, thus activating the sympathetic branch of the autonomic nervous system, preparing us to stand and fight for our lives or run like heck.

HPA

I briefly mentioned the hypothalamic-pituitary-adrenal axis earlier. When our stress response begins to shift the locus of control to the reptilian brain, our physiology reorients itself for either fight or flight. The stress response triggers the upregulating sympathetic branch of our autonomic nervous system and a part of our endocrine system known as the HPA. The hypothalamus releases a hormone known as CRH (corticotropin-releasing hormone), a so-called trigger hormone that signals the pituitary gland to release yet another hormone called ACTH (adrenocorticotropic hormone). In turn, ACTH stimulates the production and release of cortisol by the adrenal glands into the bloodstream. When cells in the hypothalamic complex detect that blood levels of cortisol are too low, the hypothalamus releases CRH as described above to increase cortisol in the bloodstream. And when the hypothalamus detects that cortisol levels are too high, it stops releasing CRH, which also means that the pituitary will stop putting out ACTH.

This negative feedback loop regulates cortisol levels for the healthy functioning of the body somewhat like how a thermostat regulates temperature in a home by turning the heating and cooling systems on and off. Since a great number of types of cells have receptors for cortisol, its levels impact parts of the body in different ways. For example, cortisol is the hormone that regulates blood sugar and metabolism.

AUTONOMIC NERVOUS SYSTEM

The flight-or-fight mechanism also operates through a part of our peripheral nervous system called the autonomic nervous system, or ANS. This part of our nervous system unconsciously manages a vast network of internal body processes that include digestion, heart and respiratory rates, sleep cycles, urinary function, and sexual response. The ANS is regulated by the hypothalamus in the limbic brain and controls the fight-or-flight response. Reflex reactions such as swallowing, coughing, and sneezing are also under the control of the ANS.

Far too many of us remain in an upregulated physiological state most of the time.

As you can see in the diagram, the ANS has two branches that are the mirror opposite of each other: the sympathetic and parasympathetic branches. Basically, the sympathetic branch upregulates our physiology, increasing our heart and respiration rates as well as pupil and bronchi dilation while pumping adrenaline, noradrenaline, and cortisol into our bloodstream and disengaging our digestive and elimination processes (which aren't immediately required for either fight or flight). The parasympathetic branch downregulates our physiology, slowing the heart and respiration rates, decreasing pupil and bronchi dilation and bringing all of our systems back online for normal functioning. At the extremes, an overactivated sympathetic response leads to a state of hyperarousal and an overactivated parasympathetic response results in a state of hypo-arousal. Generally, the sympathetic nervous system has an excitatory function and the parasympathetic system has an inhibitory or dampening function. To simplify things a bit, I'll refer to sympathetic branch activation as the *stress response* and parasympathetic branch activation as the *relaxation response*. You could also think of them as the accelerator and brake, respectively, of the ANS.

HEART RATE VARIABILITY (HRV)

Our breathing cycle forms a two-way street with our ANS. Involuntary changes in the ANS impact our breathing, but we can also regulate the ANS through conscious breathing techniques. Breathing in activates the sympathetic branch of the ANS, while breathing out correlates with parasympathetic activation. Thus, our heart rate increases slightly

Parasympathetic

Sympathetic

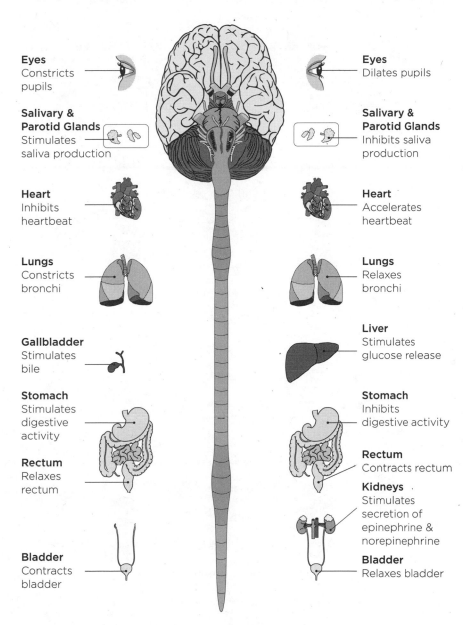

Eyes
Constricts pupils

Salivary & Parotid Glands
Stimulates saliva production

Heart
Inhibits heartbeat

Lungs
Constricts bronchi

Gallbladder
Stimulates bile

Stomach
Stimulates digestive activity

Rectum
Relaxes rectum

Bladder
Contracts bladder

Eyes
Dilates pupils

Salivary & Parotid Glands
Inhibits saliva production

Heart
Accelerates heartbeat

Lungs
Relaxes bronchi

Liver
Stimulates glucose release

Stomach
Inhibits digestive activity

Rectum
Contracts rectum

Kidneys
Stimulates secretion of epinephrine & norepinephrine

Bladder
Relaxes bladder

FIGURE 7.1 Autonomic nervous system

Autonomic Nervous System Responses

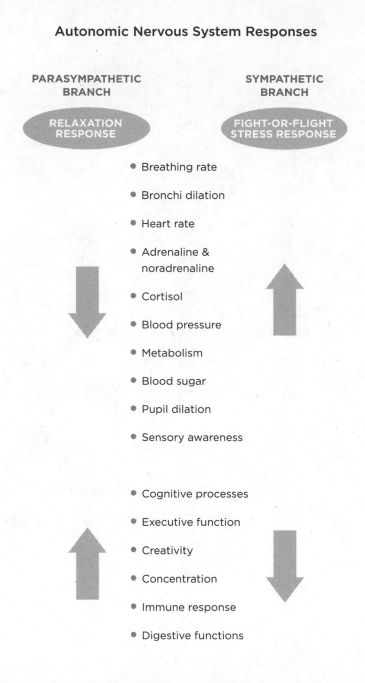

FIGURE 7.2   Relaxation response and fight-or-flight stress response

as we inhale and decreases as we exhale. This accounts for *heart rate variability* (HRV)—a good measure of healthy stress response and ANS balance. Under normal, healthy conditions, our heart rate has a natural variability following the pattern of breathing in and breathing out, but the stress response can cause us to shorten the out-breath, take rapid breaths, and rely too much on our chest muscles to breathe (rather than the diaphragm). All of this decreases HRV.

CHRONIC STRESS OR PROLONGED STRESS RESPONSE

With all of the stressors of modern living, far too many of us remain in an upregulated physiological state most of the time, either mildly or severely. This results in overactive adrenal glands and high levels of cortisol in the bloodstream, which contributes to many of the chronic stress-related health issues that keep our health-care system on the verge of breakdown:

- blood sugar imbalances such as hyperglycemia

- high blood pressure

- suppressed thyroid function

- impaired cognitive performance and short-term memory loss

- anxiety and depression

- digestive problems

- headaches

- sleep disturbances

- cardiovascular disease

- diabetes

- decreased bone density and muscle tissue

- decreased sexual response

- lowered immunity and inflammatory responses

- increased abdominal fat (correlated to all sorts of heart problems)

WHAT HAPPENED TO THE RELAXATION RESPONSE?

Why is it that we are not able to keep our autonomic nervous system in a more balanced state? I mentioned Herbert Benson and the relaxation response at the beginning of the chapter. If you have spent much time around dogs, you know how they can shift from hyperarousal (for example, barking when a stranger comes to the door) back to hypo-arousal (stretching out on the carpet fast asleep) in almost an instant. The latter is a perfect example of the relaxation response. You have probably also noticed that your napping dog breathes with its belly. This is called *diaphragmatic breathing*, a correlate of the relaxation response and parasympathetic engagement. Unlike our canine friends and other animals, we chronically stressed modern humans have simply lost the ability to relax.

We need to relearn how to engage the parasympathetic response, or ANS brake, in order to return to a normal physiological baseline when a particular stress response is no longer warranted. There is nothing wrong with the stress response, per se. In fact, it is quite necessary to our survival and crucial to meeting the challenges of contemporary life. The problem isn't stress; when properly managed, stress can actually be good for us (just as exercising—that is, *stressing*—our muscles, bones, and cardiovascular system results in obvious benefits). The problem is unmanaged, chronic stress that isn't balanced with the relaxation response.

A recent longitudinal study looked at the impact of people's beliefs about stress on health outcome and death rates. The research indicates that among people who reported high levels of stress, only those who believed stress is bad for you had higher death rates than those reporting low levels of stress. The high stress participants who did not believe stress is bad for you were no more likely to die; in fact, they had a lower death rate that those who reported low levels of stress.[4]

Health psychologist and Stanford University professor Kelly McGonigal recommends changing our attitudes about stress and developing an encouraging form of self-talk that recognizes the more positive, "rising to meet the challenge" quality of our physiological stress response when it occurs.[5] Of course, as I've suggested above, it's also incredibly important that we learn how to turn off the stress response when it is no longer warranted or helpful, and we do that by consciously engaging the parasympathetic relaxation response.

We may think of relaxation as a relatively non-alert, disengaged state that resembles or encourages sleep. Certainly this is one form of relaxation that involves the parasympathetic nervous system and is essential to getting a good night's rest. However, we can also learn to maintain a relatively alert and relaxed state that is optimal for most daily activities. The mindfulness practices presented throughout this book are designed to cultivate a baseline state of relaxed alertness as well as a balanced ANS ideal for most of the things we have to do during the day.

Let's try a couple of these practices now. Here are two simple breathing exercises that directly engage the parasympathetic branch relaxation response of the ANS.

The problem isn't stress. . . . The problem is unmanaged, chronic stress.

◀》 EXERCISE Belly Breathing

To begin with, please find a comfortable sitting posture and check to see from where you are primarily breathing, your belly or your chest. Which is rising and falling more? Many of us have become chest breathers due to chronic stress, but a more natural way of breathing uses the diaphragm muscle at the floor of the thoracic cavity. When contracted, the diaphragm creates a vacuum in the lungs, drawing in the air and pushing down on the organs in the abdominal cavity, which forces the belly out (hence, *belly* breathing). If you notice that you are breathing mostly with your chest, see if you can adjust your posture, possibly swiveling your pelvis forward, in order to switch to belly breathing. If it helps at first, place both of your hands behind your head (this disengages the muscles required for chest breathing), although I recommend doing so only until you familiarize yourself with belly breathing.

Once you have established diaphragmatic breathing, simply sit and breathe in this way. Take slightly longer and slower breaths than normal for about five minutes and notice any changes to your physiology, mood, or mental state.

If you have become a chronic chest breather, a good way to reestablish diaphragmatic breathing as your default mode is to practice belly breathing at night for five or ten minutes prior to sleep. If you can, lie on your back and place one hand on your chest and the other on your belly. Adjust your posture, especially your pelvis, until you find the hand on your belly rising and falling with the breath, while the hand on your chest remains relatively still. Simply breathe in this way, perhaps counting your breaths in cycles of ten, until you fall asleep. If you do this regularly, you can retrain yourself over time to primarily breathe from your belly. I can attest to the efficacy of this method from personal experience!

◀)) · EXERCISE   **Straw Breathing**

This exercise can be done lying down, sitting up, standing, walking, or even while driving a car (just remember to keep your eyes open!). However, for the purposes of learning this practice, please sit down and close your eyes—you can always adapt this technique later.

To begin, make sure that you are breathing primarily with your diaphragm. Now, start breathing in through your nose and out through pursed lips, as if breathing out through a straw, somewhat like whistling. (You can actually breathe through a short straw if you like, but only for the exhale.) Okay, after you've established this pattern of breathing, begin counting as you breathe in and out. For example, you might count up to four or five as you breathe in. Then extend the count and your breath a bit longer on the exhale—say, up to seven or nine. The counting is only to help you learn how to extend the out-breath several seconds or beats longer than the in-breath. Counting will also help you establish a consistent rhythm of breathing. Over time, you may wish to increase the length of both the in- and out-breath, but remain comfortable. Just breathe with your diaphragm, in through your nose, out through pursed lips, and make your out-breath about 75 to 100 percent longer than the in-breath.

Continue breathing in this way for five to ten minutes. As with the belly breathing practice, notice any changes in body or mind. If you feel dizzy or overly uncomfortable at any time, stop the practice, open your eyes, and allow your breathing pattern to return to normal.

It's important to note that when it comes to any of the practices presented in this book, ambition and strained effort are completely counterproductive. Gentleness and self-compassion are the key to working with these tools safely and successfully.

More than likely, you experienced yourself relaxing, slowing down, and feeling calmer during the last exercise. If you didn't, please don't worry; it just takes practice. And if you felt any discomfort, it may just be that this type of breathing is new for you. If so, gently try straw breathing a few times over the next several days and see if you become more comfortable with it. If it's not working for you, simply don't do it. That's why I'm offering various exercises in this book—there's something here for everyone, and you certainly don't need to do (or get good at) all of them. For those of you who might struggle with most of these exercises, don't worry; find a qualified mindfulness teacher or yoga instructor who can be a hands-on guide to helping you discover practices that work best for you.

For most people, straw breathing directly engages the relaxation response. This one simple exercise can put you in charge of your own physiology and mental state. That's a big deal, because until you learn the skills it takes to manage your internal condition, you will remain overly influenced by the world around you.

In our default mode, we tend to live in a habitually reactive state. We're at the whim of our preexisting conditioning (everything programmed into us from early childhood) and everything happening in the environment (people, situations, traffic, weather—you name it). This way of living is largely unconscious, mechanical, and ultimately unsatisfying. But there's another way. Learning simple self-management tools such as those offered in this chapter is a huge part of the path of Radical Responsibility. They are essential to helping you reclaim your personal power and develop the capacity to consciously direct your own life according to your own values, goals, and aspirations.

Neurons that fire together, wire together.
DONALD O. HEBB

8

RUTS AND GROOVES

Rewiring the Brain for Success

ost of us are aware that we have multiple conditioned behaviors that influence our daily lives to a considerable degree. We are creatures of habit, as the saying goes, and we would have a tough time getting through our day without relying on learned behaviors. We would struggle to dress ourselves or tie our shoes, much less drive a car. In fact, our very ability to walk and talk requires learned behaviors that are reflected in our neurobiological programming. All of us learn and perform a large number of life functions automatically, simply out of habit. If you don't believe this is true, try breaking a habit.

TOP-DOWN/BOTTOM-UP

Remember Paul MacLean's three-part brain theory from the previous chapter? Well, some experts such as Daniel Goleman have been using an even simpler, two-part model to help us understand the brain and its relationship to our behaviors.[1] In this model, we have on the one hand a *bottom-up brain* (I referenced this in chapter 2, describing our brain's autopilot function) that includes the brain stem, cerebellum, basal ganglia, and the limbic system (amygdala, hippocampus, thalamus, hypothalamus, and cingulate gyrus), and operates in a very programmed manner in response to various stimuli. On the other hand, we have a *top-down brain* roughly consisting of the cerebral cortex and our executive function, which impact our capacity to make mindful decisions and to consciously direct our behaviors. How many operations would you guess the bottom-up brain can perform during the same time period it takes the top-down brain to make a relatively simple decision (for example, choosing what to order for lunch)? Hundreds . . . thousands . . . millions? Actually, the bottom-up brain can perform billions of operations in the same time it takes the top-down brain to make one or two simple decisions.

Our habits, however problematic they may be, are simply learned behaviors.

The bottom-up brain has more connections and capacity than even the most advanced supercomputers today. The good news is that this ultrasupercomputer in our brain has been programmed with all kinds of helpful software, allowing us to walk and talk, get dressed, drive a car, recognize faces, and perform a host of other daily activities without having to think about it, much less relearn how to do the activities each time. Dancers, musicians, and athletes all train to perform without thinking, because thinking actually gets in the way of optimal performance.

The not-so-great news is that our bottom-up brain also relies on a lot of outdated, faulty, or downright gnarly programming—things we inherited from our family and cultural background, as well as the various survival strategies we developed in early childhood. While many of our habituated behaviors are quite necessary and useful, we also have habits that are unhealthy and harmful. Our habits may lead us to make poor diet choices, abuse alcohol, procrastinate, regularly exaggerate or tell lies, and a number of other self-defeating behaviors. Some of our habits turn into highly destructive addictions that lead us further and further into cycles of self-recrimination, self-hatred, and self-shaming.

> **EXERCISE   Healthy and Unhealthy Habits**
>
> Please open up your Radical Responsibility journal and write "Healthy Habits" at the top of one page and "Unhealthy Habits" at the top of another. List as many habits as you can under each category. Without judgment or blame of any kind, reflect on what you have written down. Take a moment to really appreciate the healthy habits you have identified, and then reflect on how helpful it would be to let go of some of the unhealthy ones. This chapter will give you the skills to begin doing just that.

What are we to do about the ingrained habits that keep getting in our way despite our best intentions (and repeated commitments) to behave otherwise? First of all, it is very helpful to remember the truth of our innate worthiness, and to realize that our habits, however problematic they may be, are simply learned behaviors. Every single one of them originated from the collective impact of the survival-focused human condition we are all challenged to both embrace and transcend. It's also helpful to realize that our habits are reflected in the neural pathways and networks in our brain, which, despite being deeply ingrained, are nonetheless changeable. These neural pathways can be associated with particular triggering stimuli coming from any of our senses, and they can also be state-specific—meaning they are associated with a specific mental or emotional state. For example, you've likely experienced yourself salivating over the smell of foods such as french fries or popcorn. And you've also likely noticed that this effect is stronger or weaker depending on your state of mind and how hungry you are.

NEUROPLASTICITY: OUR BRAIN'S AMAZING CAPACITY TO CHANGE

You've probably heard the adage that you can't teach an old dog new tricks. Well, as it turns out, current science says you can, though the older the dog, the more effort it may require. Habits can be deeply engrained. We acquired most of them in childhood and have been reinforcing them ever since. Even though we may come to recognize many of our shortcomings, emotional triggers, and problematic behaviors for what they are—old childhood coping strategies that no longer serve us—they can still prove incredibly difficult to change. Likewise, simply gaining more scientific knowledge about the brain will not in itself change our habits or significantly impact the course of our lives. However, if we are willing to apply this knowledge and employ various body-mind practices (such as mindfulness meditation) to rewire the neurobiological structure of our brains, we can, in fact, replace old habits with new ones and change our lives for the better.

We're each destined to become the captain of our own vessel, and we can do so by taking ownership of our own brain.

Contrary to popular belief, our brains do not own us. We're not slaves to old habits, and we're not at the mercy of synapses gone haywire. In truth, we're each destined to become the captain of our own vessel, and we can do so by taking ownership of our own brain. We can create new neural networks that support a shift in consciousness from victimhood to ownership. If we're willing to step up and learn the skills and practices needed to be a responsible owner of this incredibly complex, biochemical-electrical supercomputer sitting on our shoulders, we can direct our own destiny in ways that many would consider impossible. At the very least, we can set ourselves back on course to fulfilling our aspirations and dreams.

REWIRING THE BRAIN

During my early prison years, I had the opportunity to study computer programming. The prison education department where I worked as a teacher had the early personal computers used in many schools, the Apple IIe. We only had access to them during class time in the computer lab, but we could take printouts of the programs we were writing back to our housing units to work on in the evenings or on weekends.

I remember lying on my bunk, reading one of these programs and trying to make sense of the algorithms and coding I had written. I would struggle to understand the program and visualize the operations I intended it to perform. I would literally feel my brain clouding up so badly that I felt slightly disoriented with a mild headache. As I stuck with it, though, this state of mental confusion and physical suffering would eventually give way to an amazing clarity, and I would suddenly find myself understanding the program in an entirely new way. I had this experience frequently enough to become quite curious about it. When it happened, I could literally feel my brain going through some kind of physical change. I had an intuitive sense that I was altering the neural pathways in the brain through my intense effort to understand the abstractions of this early computer language while visualizing the operations the program code would produce.

At that point in the late 1980s, neuroplasticity was barely on the horizon, and it didn't fully emerge as established science until a decade later. Basically, neuroplasticity describes the ability of the brain to restructure itself and form new neuronal connections and neural pathways. For better or worse, the brain is continually restructuring itself based on how we use it, how we take care of our physical health, and the particular stimuli to which we expose it.

In other words, we're not stuck with the brain with which we entered adulthood, nor are we fated to experience aging-related brain deterioration in our later years. We now know that our brains can thrive throughout our life span if we take care of our health and challenge our brains through continual learning, especially the kind that requires the formation of new neural pathways (such as learning a new language—Apple Basic, for example).

Neuroplasticity, however, is not all good news. Our brains are in a continual process of restructuring based on the richness or poverty of our environment. If we sit on the couch all day watching reality TV, well, that's going to change what's going on upstairs, and probably not for the better. So based on what we know now about neuroplasticity, we would all be better served to expose our brains to all the enriching information we can access while avoiding negativity and superficial entertainment as much as possible.

———————————— **Neuroscience Note** ————————————

Physical exercise and basic mindfulness practice (see chapter 2) have both been shown to significantly enhance neuroplasticity and cognitive performance in the brain.[2]

The healthy functioning of our brain impacts every aspect of our quality of life, including the mental, emotional, relational, and spiritual dimensions. It affects our moment-to-moment experience of ourselves and the world around us, our performance of mental and physical tasks, the quality of our communication, our relationships with others, and the effectiveness with which we meet the challenges of life. Our brain also impacts our ability to make moral and ethical decisions and to have a healthy social and spiritual life.

Despite all the advances in our knowledge of the human brain, we appear to be experiencing a pandemic of brain-based disorders likely related to the unfortunate facts of modern life: chronic stress, pollution, chemical and electromagnetic exposure of all kinds, processed and genetically modified foods, radio waves, radioactivity, and continual exposure to our numerous digital devices. Sadly, attention deficit hyperactivity disorder (ADHD), anxiety, depression, and addictive-compulsive disorders, as well as Alzheimer's and other forms of dementia are all on the rise.

We may be more challenged than ever before in human history to safeguard our health, especially the healthy functioning of our brains. Fortunately, there is compelling scientific evidence that we can actually improve brain health and function throughout the course of our lives.[3] First of all, what's good for the body is good for the brain—healthy nutrition (non-GMO, antibiotic-free, organic, unprocessed whole foods), regular exercise (aerobic and anaerobic), proper hydration, sufficient oxygenation (through diaphragmatic breathing), and limited exposure to environmental pollutants and toxins. More specifically, the mindfulness practices in chapter 2 and the compassion practices in chapter 13, as well as other mental challenge and learning activities, directly support and enhance brain health and performance.[4]

HABIT FORMATION

The science of habit formation has advanced steadily during the past several decades, and a quick online search will yield a host of recent books on the subject, with business writer Charles Duhigg's *The Power of Habit* among the most widely recommended. Of course, it's beyond the scope of this chapter to summarize that material, but I do want to offer some tools to help you transform your brain and optimize its performance to get back into the driver's seat of your own life.

The basics are fairly simple: Repeating certain behaviors again and again over time will train your brain to habitually produce those behaviors. As well, consistently boycotting particular habitual behaviors over time will gradually weaken those habits. Further, repeating an alternative behavior again and again will eventually form a new habit. Habit formation follows a three-step feedback loop (sometimes called the habit loop) consisting of: (1) a cue or trigger, (2) a behavior or routine, and (3) a reward (see figure 8.1).

Understanding these mechanics can help us hack the brain's habitual behavior systems in order to reduce the influence of unhealthy habits and replace them with powerful new behaviors designed to create the results we want in life.

So how exactly does the habit loop work? When we experience a given trigger or cue, we respond (consciously or unconsciously) with a particular behavior that leads to a reward or payoff of some kind. The next time we experience the trigger, we repeat the same behavior expecting the same reward. Our desire, or *craving*, for the reward is what drives the habit loop and the process of habit formation.

We know about the neuromechanics of craving from decades of research in the field of alcohol and drug addiction treatment. Our habitual behaviors and related emotional states not only have underlying neural pathways but are also correlated with particular chemical balances in our brain. We could think of these chemical balances as neurochemical comfort zones. Once our brain has become habituated to a particular neurochemical mix, changes to that balance trigger the experience of craving—the impulse to return to our comfort zone. The experience of craving is actually part of a natural physiological process known as homeostasis; it's how living organisms maintain stable states, or equilibrium.

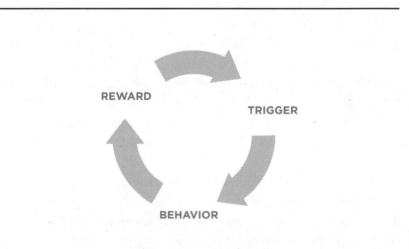

FIGURE 8.1 The habit loop

For example, let's say that while working at my computer and trying to concentrate, I experience an uncomfortable drop in energy and sensations of hunger, so I consume an energy-boosting snack of some kind. My hunger goes away, my energy level is restored (homeostasis), and I'm able to focus on my work again. Here's how that looks on the habit loop:

Trigger (cue)   drop in energy, loss of focus,
                     hunger sensations

Behavior (routine)   eating an energy-boosting snack

Reward (payoff)   energy renewed, focus returns,
                       hunger suppressed

Sooner or later, the energy-boosting and hunger-suppressing effect of the snack wears off. When that happens, I experience the trigger again and the accompanying craving for a snack (or the payoff promised by the snack). The cycle repeats itself, and each time I reach for the snack and experience the expected reward, I reinforce the new habit pattern. I start stashing snacks in my desk and briefcase, now convinced that I can't get through a morning or afternoon at work without them.

I'm stuck in a rut. He's in the groove. She's on the right track. These familiar metaphors have been around for a long time, well before the advent of modern neuroscience—a strong indication that we have an intuitive sense of how our brain works. Our habitual behaviors and their underlying neuronal structures are very much like physical ruts and grooves in the brain. We generally associate *ruts*—like those in a poorly maintained dirt road—with bad habits, and *grooves*—like those on our favorite jazz record—with good habits. Jazz musicians in the 1920s coined the expression "in the groove," and decades later "groovy" became an iconic expression of the hippie movement. Today we still talk about "getting our groove on."

Neural pathways are like the roads we use commuting to and from work, shopping for groceries, traveling to the gym, and so on. We all have certain routes that have become so habitual we could almost do them without thinking. As I mentioned in chapter 2, our bottom-up brain is capable of driving a car even when our top-down brain is paying less than optimal attention.

So let's say that you're driving down the highway and come to that exit with the drive-through Starbucks just off the exit ramp. If, like me, caffeine is your drug of choice and Starbucks is one of your well-*grooved* habit loops, you may almost feel the car veering toward that exit all on its own. In your java-oriented perception, that exit ramp looks and feels more like a turnoff to heaven than a normal highway exit. We've all experienced these kinds of highly programmed auto-pilot behaviors. That pull or momentum we feel toward a particular behavior is literally the activation of a neural structure in our brain that operates much like a familiar roadway.

"Neurons that fire together, wire together," an insight from Canadian neuropsychologist Donald O. Hebb, means that repeated behaviors or associations lead to various changes in the brain's neuronal structures, forming the neurobiological basis for learning and habit formation. Cells paired in repeated synaptic firing will form neural networks that organize numerous brain operations for efficient automaticity.

The ability to *groove* that perfect golf swing, for example, comes down to repeating the same behaviors, under the same conditions, again and again—practice, practice, practice. Most expert golfers have developed a consistent pre-swing routine, including a particular move-ment, however subtle (the cue), with which they initiate the swing (the behavior) precisely the same way every time, producing a fluid swing without thinking and the kind of golf shots that are the dream (reward) of every golfer.

The difference between the erratic weekend player and the con-sistent professional golfer is simply the extent to which they have or have not *grooved* the necessary swing mechanics for particular golf shots through frequent repetition of the desired behavior—practice makes perfect. The weekend player likely has neural networks and the muscle memory for good golf shots, and they may even manage to pull off a few great shots here and there. The problem is that the neural pathways are weak and don't provide the golfer with suffi-cient confidence. So more often than not, they allow their thinking mind to get involved, attempting to consciously steer the shot in the desired direction—an awkward approach that generally spells disaster. In contrast, the professional golfer analyzes the situation, selects the proper club, decides on a particular approach to the shot, and simply follows their well-practiced routine, making a conscious effort to *disengage* the thinking brain. This approach allows the bottom-up brain to fluidly execute the stroke by following a robust, deeply-grooved neural pathway to success.

We can change habits, even highly addictive ones such as smoking.

Unfortunately, our bad habits can also be deeply ingrained in our neuronal structures, but even those pathways require regular upkeep and maintenance, just like the roads we use to get to work. Remember Hebb's statement: "Neurons that fire together, wire together." It's also true that neurons that stop firing together, cease wiring together. This is how we can weaken less-than-ideal neural pathways over time.

We know from functional MRI brain research studies with practitioners of mindfulness-based stress reduction (MBSR) and other forms of mindfulness, that we can change neural pathways by directing our mental and emotional focus in certain ways.[5] Here's an example: The kind of mind training taught in a basic MBSR course involves self-regulating one's wandering attention back to the breath again and again (as you learned to do in chapter 2). Mindfulness practitioners are actually interrupting habitual patterns of discursiveness and distraction by intentional *attention switching*—consciously bringing their attention back to a chosen object of mindfulness (in this case, the physical sensations of breathing).

When a habit's underlying neural pathways go unused and the neurons cease firing together, the neural tracks atrophy to some degree and it becomes easier to suppress an undesirable habitual behavior and replace it with another. Unfortunately, the neural pathways and networks underlying our habits don't go away completely, but more on that later. However, understanding the science of habit formation can empower us to change or eliminate habits that are no longer serving us. We can also form new habits that will get us where we want to go.

Set yourself up for success. Public health and environmental education programs (such as smoking cessation and recycling campaigns) are designed to inspire and support large numbers of people in changing their habits, typically by enticing them to exchange old identities for new ones that come with higher social approval, which also means a higher level of self-validation payoff. The important lesson here is that we *can* change habits, even highly addictive ones such as smoking. And when we connect new behaviors and rewards to some form of self-validation, it turbocharges the craving that successfully drives any new habit loop.

Okay, we now have greater insight into the process of habit formation—the three-part habit loop. We also know that our habits have neurobiological underpinnings that operate much like our systems of roads and highways. Furthermore, we know that repeating a behavior strengthens a habit by reinforcing its underlying neural pathways and that boycotting a behavior weakens a habit by impairing its pathways. We might not understand the origins of the ruts we sometimes find ourselves in, but we at least know how and why the ruts get deeper over time. Finally, we now have some knowledge about how to escape those ruts and consciously *groove* new behaviors in order to direct our lives in more positive directions. Armed with this information, we can now form a twofold strategy for replacing undesirable habits with more desirable ones:

1. Boycott the old habitual reaction to a particular cue or trigger.

2. Implement a new habit loop designed to establish a new response to the same trigger.

Let's return to the example I used earlier about my former habit of snacking at work. Here's how that habit loop goes:

Trigger (cue)   drop in energy, loss of focus,
                         hunger sensations

Behavior (routine)   eating an energy-boosting snack

Reward (payoff)   energy renewed, focus returns,
                         hunger suppressed

So to change this habit, the strategy is to boycott the old behavior (rut) and establish a new, more desirable one (groove) in response to the same trigger. The new habit loop looks like this:

Trigger (cue)   drop in energy, loss of focus, hunger pangs

Behavior (routine)   stand, stretch, breathe deeply,
                             drink a glass of water, stretch
                             more, and return to work

Reward (payoff)   energy comes back, focus returns,
                         hunger goes away

You will notice that both the trigger and the reward are exactly the same. The only thing we have changed here is the behavior in response to the trigger. Of course, it's absolutely critical that the new behavior actually produces the reward, and the reward should be compelling enough to trigger craving for it. Remember that *craving the reward* is what fuels the habit loop and the process of new habit formation.

There is one other important difference between the old and the new habit loops. While they both lead to the same short-term reward—a return to normal energy levels and capacity for concentration—they each lead to different long-term outcomes. The old habit in this example leads to feelings of being addicted and not in control of one's behavior (with the added possibilities of digestive, overeating, and weight gain issues), as well as the accompanying sensations of shame and unworthiness. The replacement habit loop, however, leads to a sense of control, self-mastery, self-worth, improved digestion, better weight management, and a much-improved long-term health outlook. Those are substantially different results. The latter can even involve a new identity as someone who is health conscious, in control, and self-confident. The rewards of that new identity and the social approval associated with it will enhance the craving factor driving the habit loop even more, thereby grooving the new behavior in the form of an established neural pathway.

EXERCISE   Habit Transformation

Start a new page in your Radical Responsibility journal with the heading "Habit Transformation." Reflect on one of your less desirable habits, one that undermines your effectiveness or quality of life in some way. It's also a good idea to choose a negative habit in which you can clearly see all of the elements of the habit loop. In your journal, write down the trigger, behavior, and reward of that particular habit. Then reflect on a healthier replacement for the behavior, one that responds to the same trigger and leads to the same—or an even more powerful—reward. Once you're clear on the replacement behavior and the new habit loop, begin experimenting with enacting it right away.

Return to your Radical Responsibility journal periodically to note your progress. Once you have success with this method of habit transformation, you will likely want to apply it to other not-so-helpful habits. If you struggle too much with the habit you chose to work on, try a different one. Perhaps choose another habit that feels a little easier or less deeply embedded. The important thing is to experience confidence in your ability to transform habits in this way.

We commonly hear that it takes ninety days to establish a lifelong habit, but the research is less clear. Health psychology researcher Phillippa Lally and colleagues recently studied ninety-six participants who were attempting to establish new habits, some as simple as drinking a glass of water before lunch or running for fifteen minutes before dinner. The researchers found that the time it took for participants to establish the new habit ranged anywhere from 18 to 254 days (and 66 days on average).[6] There's a silver lining to this news: if it does actually take up to eight months to fully establish a new habit, we can relax and let go of any expectations of overnight success. We can instead focus on long-term gains. Fortunately, some new behaviors (such as a new workout routine or a regular mindfulness practice) provide immediate rewards while also increasing the likelihood of longer term benefits along the way.

The important thing is to stick with it and never give up. It's also essential to set yourself up for success. Make sure that new behaviors fit into your daily or weekly routines, give yourself adequate time to do them, set up effective reminders, and rely on a buddy or find a community for support. And remember that the old neural pathways are still there, which means that relapses are normal and quite likely to occur. It's important to inoculate yourself ahead of time against letting a relapse send you into a tailspin of self-loathing and compensatory acting out. It's also helpful to develop a "no big deal" attitude toward relapses. Just think of them as road bumps and useful reminders to redouble your efforts to establish the new positive habit. Remember: if you stick with a new behavior long enough, it will become neurologically robust and therefore easily sustainable.

MIND TRAINING, NEUROPLASTICITY, AND HEALTHY BRAIN FUNCTION

In summary, we can significantly enhance our quality of life and overall physical, mental, emotional, and spiritual health by regularly practicing mindfulness, replacing unhealthy habits with healthy ones, and increasing our propensity to have a caring, empathic, and compassionate relationship with ourselves and others.

Functional MRI brain scans show that various forms of mind training—mindfulness, for example—can actually change the physical structure of the brain.[7] Mind training can be as simple as deliberately bringing your attention to whatever physical sensations you're having in the moment. I mentioned the benefits of MBSR above. Well, participation in MBSR courses (commonly structured as eight, two-hour weekly classes with a day of mindfulness and a daily practice commitment) has been correlated with measurable increases in gray matter in the frontal lobe regions of the brain—the region involved in attention and emotion regulation—and in white matter myelination (which supports more efficient brain function overall).[8]

I'm not going to attempt to summarize the vast body of current research on mindfulness practices here—there were over one thousand published studies on mindfulness in 2017 alone. Instead, I recommend that you read *Altered Traits: Science Reveals How Meditation Changes Your Mind, Brain, and Body* by Daniel Goleman and Richard Davidson. They've done an excellent job of distilling the best current research on mindfulness and meditation for a lay audience, applying rigorous standards to the studies they included. Goleman and Davidson conclude that mindfulness meditation practices do indeed make numerous contributions to developing a healthier body and mind, noting four areas of particular benefit or improvement related to specific neuronal structures amenable to change:

- reacting to disturbing events, experiencing stress, and recovery from stress

- feeling empathy and compassion

- regulating attention

- experiencing our sense of self, or *self-sense*[9]

Creating new neural pathways to replace unhealthy habits or enhance your brain's capacities isn't rocket science, as they say. It's just a matter of taking action with some of the strategies outlined in this chapter.

The keys are consistency, trusting in yourself, and being open to new possibilities. And it will be far easier if you create new habits that are meaningful, fun, or exciting, ones that resonate with you emotionally. I would also encourage you to marshal your courage to try new behaviors that challenge your assumed limitations and ingrained fears.

You can also create entirely new habits that have absolutely nothing to do with old habits you are trying to break. Learn a new language. Take up a new hobby. Learn to paint or play a musical instrument of some kind. Above all, remember that life is full of

> When you stumble, just get back up, dust yourself off with self-compassion and humor, and keep going.

infinite possibilities. When you stumble, just get back up, dust yourself off with self-compassion and humor, and keep going. Life is too short to agonize about the past! The next moment, the next adventure, is always arising—right here, right now.

PART IV

EMBRACING THE PATH OF RADICAL RESPONSIBILITY

What I learned at a very early age was that I was responsible for my life. And as I became more spiritually conscious, I learned that we all are responsible for ourselves, that you create your own reality by the way you think and therefore act. You cannot blame apartheid, your parents, your circumstances, because you are not your circumstances. You are your possibilities. If you know that, you can do anything. **OPRAH WINFREY**

9

TRANSFORMING THE VICTIM MINDSET

In this chapter we will begin to explore the Empowerment Zone/ Drama Zone distinction at the very heart of the Radical Responsibility approach to living with authenticity and genuine personal power. In short, we'll reclaim our freedom and agency even further by investigating the way we choose—consciously or unconsciously—to perceive, think, and feel about the external circumstances we encounter in our day-to-day lives. In short, the *Empowerment Zone* is a life context defined by what I call a *responsive-relational mode* of being and interacting that creates limitless possibility and authentic relationship. In contrast, the *Drama Zone* is a context characterized *reactive-survival mode* that creates endless constriction, conflict, and suffering.

Many of us who have worked in organizations of various sizes have witnessed how badly people can behave when they're seeking approval or vying for status and power in a perceived hierarchical system. This is especially true if the organization encourages competitiveness in the context of a fear-based, survival-of-the-fittest organizational culture (not so different from a reality TV show premise such as *Survivor*).

Much to our dismay, we may have even found ourselves getting caught up in such survival behaviors to one degree or another.

Gossip, backbiting, blame, and negative politics too often plague organizational cultures. Some employees even engage in proactively undermining others who they perceive as standing in their way or threatening their status or power in some way. They may do this on their own or forge Drama Triangle alliances with other coworkers to sabotage perceived adversaries or drive them out of the organization all together. Sadly, too many employees resign themselves to working in companies where they have to watch their backs and play politics to one degree or another simply to survive, much less advance in the enterprise.

It doesn't have to be this way. However, if leaders don't work to establish a different kind of environment, the default culture will tend to be fear-based and prone to unhealthy drama. As I posited in chapters 4 and 5, that's the default setup for all of us to one degree or another. The negative core beliefs we have inherited and developed, combined with the impact of the negativity bias explored in chapter 7, lead us to depend on fear-based and often underhanded strategies for getting our needs met. In organizational life, power and status are extremely important to most of us, whether we know it or not. When those needs—along with the others discussed in the SCARF model presented in chapter 3—are threatened or unmet, we typically react physiologically as if our own lives were threatened.

There is no in-between or gray area here.

Of course, we experience similar dynamics in our personal lives as well. Anytime we perceive our needs for food, warmth, shelter, financial security, status, relatedness, autonomy, inclusion, love, fairness, and so on, as being at risk, we are in danger of the survival-focused reptilian brain assuming control. How many times have we seen someone (or ourselves) reacting to ordinary daily challenges at home or at work as if their very life were at stake? This occurs when the relatively hardwired survival strategies and adaptations we learned in early life kick in and take over.

OUR VICTIM NARRATIVES

The following exercise may be one of the most important exercises you do on your Radical Responsibility journey (or in your entire life, for that matter). It's crucial to directly experience the Empowerment Zone/Drama Zone distinction, which is one of the key life distinctions in the Radical Responsibility philosophy and way of life. *Life distinctions* (sometimes called *training distinctions*) are sharp-edged dichotomies, such as being an optimist or pessimist—seeing the glass half full or half empty. There is no in-between or gray area here, and it's the clear-cut nature of these distinctions (whether artificial or not) that give them the power to leverage transformation. So when it comes to the Empowerment Zone/Drama Zone life distinction, there is no middle ground. There's an identifiable boundary, and you can use this schema to locate your position in one zone or the other at any given moment.

Please take your time to thoroughly engage this exercise and be sure to make notes on your experience in your Radical Responsibility journal.

◀)) **EXERCISE** **Victim Story**

Okay, please take a comfortable seat. First, close your eyes and bring your attention to your body, to the actual tactile physical sensations that make up your moment-to-moment experience of being alive right now. If your attention wanders, gently bring it back to the body. Allow this gentle and persistent attentiveness to the moment-to-moment experience of being alive in your body to gradually stabilize you in a present moment awareness. If you like, you can also focus on your breathing and all the particular physical sensations that arise and fall away in the body with each inhalation and exhalation. Do this for two or three minutes, or until you feel relatively present and "in your body." We are going to explore the depths of the victim mindset from the Drama Triangle (chapters 5 and 6), and the more present you are, the more you will learn.

To continue, please reflect on a situation in your adult life. Don't choose something from your childhood but rather something that happened as an adult (the more recent, the better) when you felt victimized or taken advantage of in some way—basically when you were mistreated or you got a bum deal. You may have moved on, but at the time you were quite outraged and had a lot of clarity about your innocence, as well as the culpability of whoever the perceived perpetrator (persecutor) was. In fact, at that moment, you could have been the greatest prosecuting attorney in the world, and the perp would have rightly received the maximum sentence. Some part of your brain was convinced that this was a crime against humanity itself, and it deserved swift and severe justice. Okay, that may be a bit over the top, but you get the idea.

If you have actually been seriously violated in some way as an adult, please don't choose to work with that experience. Pick a situation you can reasonably deal with on your own. Perhaps one of the more garden-variety occurrences of feeling disrespected, taken advantage of, betrayed, or lied to that likely had you quite outraged and upset at the time.

Once you've selected the experience, do your best to bring it alive as if it had just happened. Begin sharing it verbally or silently with some imagined person. Whoever it is, I want you to go all out in convincing them of your victimization. Basically, your goal is to turn that person into your enthusiastic and impassioned rescuer, and try to play it up as if you actually need rescuing. It's important to go all out here, because getting these life distinctions in your bones is the key that opens the door to genuine freedom and real transformation.

Just to give you a sense of the urgency with which I'm inviting you to engage in this learning exercise, imagine that you're an innocent tourist who has been falsely accused and imprisoned in a foreign country. The prison conditions are the worst imaginable. You've been awaiting trial for months, fighting off the cockroaches, rats, and your fellow prisoners. You're at the end of your rope, entirely desperate. Suddenly a somewhat wimpy-looking consulate officer from the US Embassy stops by your cell. You have three minutes to get them on your side. If you fail, you will likely rot in this prison for years.

That's how serious you should play this. Feel the experience of victimization flood your mind and body with all the vivid storylines, details, and accompanying feelings. Now imagine that you have called your spouse, best friend, or whoever you might likely download this experience to with the expectation of their sympathy and understanding. That's where the three minutes come in. You have only that amount of time to thoroughly convince this imagined person that you were truly and outrageously victimized. Please set a timer on your cell phone or watch, press start when you're ready, and let the person know all about it. By the time you finish, your imagined partner should be even more outraged than you and ready to go after the perp(s)! So hold nothing back and engage this exercise as if your life depends on it, because in a real sense, it does.

When your time's up, be sure to stop. If you're like most people, that's hard to do, because once you get on a roll you want to keep going. Make sure you keep to the time limit, and when it's time to stop, close your eyes and just notice how you feel in your body. What does it feel like physically and emotionally to be so immersed in this story of victimization? Getting to know the physiological state and embodied experience associated with the victim mindset is critical to getting free from the grip of victim-thinking and drama. Just stay with your experience for a moment and be curious. The point is to become very familiar with the physiological and emotional landscape of the victim mindset.

Now, please reflect on the story you just told to an imagined friend. What were the themes of this particular victim narrative? Common themes include injustice, betrayal, abuse of power, being taken advantage of, deception, dishonesty, disrespect, the incompetency of others, violation of trust, broken agreements, being passed over or undervalued, and so forth. What were the key themes in your story of victimization? Write down as many themes as you can identify in your Radical Responsibility journal.

Now let's shift from themes to feelings. As you retold this victim story, what feelings arose? Even more importantly, think about all the emotions you experienced when the event actually occurred. Feelings associated with victimization usually include fear, anxiety, hurt, anger, rage, sadness, shock, disbelief, overwhelm, helplessness, powerlessness, hopelessness, despair, shame, guilt, and so on. What emotions were present for you? Write down as many feelings as you can remember.

Look at figure 9.1 below. How many of the themes and feelings outlined there are familiar to you or were present in your story?

Drama Zone			
THEMES		**FEELINGS**	
• Injustice	• Deception	• Fear	• Shame
• Betrayal	• Incompetence	• Anger	• Guilt
• Abuse of power	• Unfairness	• Hurt	• Vengefulness
• Exploitation	• Unseen/not validated	• Confusion	• Sadness
• Misunderstanding	• Unfairly passed over	• Shock	• Powerlessness
• Disrespect	• Bias, prejudice	• Disbelief	• Hopelessness
• Broken agreements	• Bigotry	• Overwhelmed	• Despair
• Violation of trust	• Racism	• Frozen	• Anxiety
• Dishonesty	• Politics	• Rage	• Numbness
	• Distrust	• Disappointment	• Isolation
	• Oppression		

FIGURE 9.1 Drama Zone themes and feelings

OWNERSHIP NARRATIVE

Okay, now we're going to do something a bit more challenging. We're going to retell our victim story from the perspective of accountability and ownership. That means I want you to look back at the circumstances behind your victim story and see if you can own something about it. What part—no matter how small—did you play in its creation?

I want to offer a little rubric to help you out here. I call it the CPA. Certified public accountants are all about accountability, but I'm using the CPA acronym a little differently here:

- *C* stands for *caused it* or *contributed to it.* Can you find any way in which you caused or contributed to the circumstances that underlie the victim story you told earlier? As the saying goes, it takes two to tango. What part did you have in the dance?

- *P* stands for *promoted it.* Reexamine your victim narrative and look for how you might have set yourself up by replaying unconscious scripts from your past. Often when something happens in our early childhood that causes us to feel unsafe or overwhelms our fragile and limited coping skills, we create a story to make sense of things. The departure of a divorcing parent early in childhood could leave us with the story that "anyone I really love and need abandons me" or "my mother or father left because I'm a bad person, unworthy and unlovable." Transactional analysis calls these stories *life scripts.* They become psychologically and neurobiologically ingrained in us at an early age, and we tend to play the stories out over and over again. Basically, the idea is that in adulthood we're constantly trying to prove that the conclusions we made about our circumstances in childhood—those that we've built our identity around—are true. This provides one explanation for why people repeat the same types of dysfunctional relationships, habitually get fired from jobs for similar reasons, or replay other harmful patterns throughout the course of their lives. So I invite you to think about your story with this in mind. What life scripts might have been involved, with or without your knowledge at the time?

- *A* stands for *allowed it.* We can allow circumstances to occur for any number of reasons: poor boundaries, lack of assertiveness, conflict avoidance, poor communication, faulty due diligence, or inattentiveness. What's your tendency? How might you have allowed your victim story to play out in the first place?

◀)) **EXERCISE** **Taking Accountability**

Now that you're familiar with the CPA tool, let's apply it to the circumstance and victim story you worked with above. See if you can identify some way in which you caused it, contributed to it, promoted it, or allowed it. Here's your opportunity to own something and take your power back. Dig into the circumstances behind your story and see if you can find anything—anything at all—to own. Even if you just barely crack open the door of ownership and accountability, that's a start. Just begin there and see where it takes you. Focus on telling a new story, creating a new narrative from the perspective of Radical Responsibility. Oh, and one more thing—make sure you use the correct pronoun when doing so. In other words, be sure to speak in *I* statements.

I want to remind you that this exercise (and any of the others in this book) has nothing to do with blaming yourself. It's also not about beating yourself up. On the contrary, taking ownership is an act of self-compassion. It's the key to learning about ourselves and developing the ability to make conscious, healthy, and more beneficial choices.

So let's do it. Set your timer for three minutes again, but this time tell a different story to a different friend—the kind of friend who will hold you more accountable and call your victim mindset into question. Remember the CPA rubric—find your doorway into ownership, anything at all that you can own, and go!

Okay, when your three minutes are up, once again close your eyes and just notice how it feels in your body to be making this type of shift (or at least trying to). Just stay with the physical sensations for a moment. Training yourself to clearly recognize how the mindset of ownership and accountability feels different in your body from the experience of being immersed in the victim mindset is a critical step to freeing yourself from the grip of victim-thinking and drama.

Next, please reflect on this new version of the story you just told to an imagined friend. What were some of the themes of ownership or accountability in this story? Perhaps you recognized that you were enabling someone else, rescuing them, or simply people pleasing. Maybe you see that there was actually something in it for you. Or perhaps you now notice how your poor boundaries, lazy communication, or not following through with something important contributed to the situation. What are the themes of ownership in this new accountable version of your story? Write them down in your Radical Responsibility journal—we'll come back to them in a moment.

Now, as we did in the earlier exercise, I want you to pay attention to any feelings that came up as you made the effort to shift from the victim mindset to accountability. Common feelings associated with embracing ownership are clarity, relief, empowerment or less powerlessness, empathy, compassion, regret, embarrassment, confusion, maturity, peacefulness, calmness, humor, and so on. What feelings or emotions were present for you? How did it feel different, if it did, from when you were completely immersed in the victim story? Again, please grab your Radical Responsibility journal and write down as many feelings or emotions as you can remember experiencing while you told your accountable version of the story.

Now look at the upper half of figure 9.2 on the next page. How many of the themes and feelings outlined there came up for you in the telling of the accountable version of your story? I imagine you would agree that this is a markedly different landscape from the one you created earlier from the victim mindset. ·

THEMES		FEELINGS	
• Accountability	• I wasn't paying	• Challenged	• Learning
• Responsibility	attention	• Confusion	• Understanding
• Ownership	• I didn't do my	• Empowerment	• Maturity
• I was: enabling	due diligence	• Less helpless	• Disorientation
colluding,	• I could have	• Clarity	• Hopefulness
rescuing,	seen it coming	• Calm	• Openness
people-	• I did see	• Peace	• Stability
pleasing,	it coming	• Empathy	• Wisdom
distracted,	• I ignored	• Compassion	• Reasonableness
unaware,	that quiet	• Regret	• Capableness
lazy, conflict	voice within	• Embarrassment	• Resilience
avoidant	• I didn't	• Relief	
• I had poor	speak up		
boundaries	• I was in denial		

Empowerment Zone
OWNERSHIP STORY: RESPONSIBILITY

Drama Zone
VICTIM STORY: BLAME

THEMES		FEELINGS	
• Injustice	• Deception	• Fear	• Shame
• Betrayal	• Incompetence	• Anger	• Guilt
• Abuse of	• Unfairness	• Hurt	• Vengefulness
power	• Unseen/not	• Confusion	• Sadness
• Exploitation	validated	• Shock	• Powerlessness
• Misunder-	• Unfairly	• Disbelief	• Hopelessness
standing	passed over	• Overwhelmed	• Despair
• Disrespect	• Bias, prejudice	• Frozen	• Anxiety
• Broken	• Bigotry	• Rage	• Numbness
agreements	• Racism	• Disappointment	• Isolation
• Violation	• Politics		
of trust	• Distrust		
• Dishonesty	• Oppression		

FIGURE 9.2 Empowerment Zone themes and feelings

It's not that the Empowerment Zone landscape is a rose garden. It can prove quite challenging to admit our part in things, and doing so can bring up uncomfortable feelings. But just notice how different the two sets of themes and feelings are. Most of us are likely clear about which landscape we'd prefer!

Sometimes, participants in my Radical Responsibility trainings struggle with feelings of guilt or shame when they recognize their part in creating a particular drama or conflict. It's natural to feel some regret or embarrassment when claiming our part in a painful dynamic, but guilt and shame are not helpful because they involve self-blame and take us right back to the Drama Zone again. Remember, you can recognize the impact you've had on others and at the same time generate kindness and compassion for everyone involved—including yourself.

OWNERSHIP VERSUS BLAME

As I mentioned above, being accountable has nothing to do with blame. Blame lands you back in the Drama Zone, whether you're blaming others or yourself. Taking ownership and accountability simply means that you see your part in interpersonal dynamics, and that radical act empowers you to make new choices in the future. You're freeing yourself from the grip of old patterns—jettisoning the outdated behaviors that no longer serve you. This means that you can now choose how to respond to any given circumstance and that you own the consequences of your choices. And even when you can't see that you had anything to do with causing, promoting, or allowing an unfortunate interaction or experience, you can still take ownership for how you choose to respond to that circumstance.

> You can now choose how to respond to any given circumstance.

Freeing ourselves from the blame paradigm isn't easy. We have all been enculturated to believe that someone *must* be to blame when things go wrong. Additionally, most of us have experienced plenty of blame and its close cousin *shame* in our lives, and we would rather do anything than set ourselves up to deal with those painful feelings again. Quite naturally—and almost instinctually—we blame others to protect that soft, tender, and vulnerable place in our heart that has been bruised repeatedly in childhood and since. But it won't help to blame ourselves for blaming! We just do our best to recognize this completely human tendency in ourselves with self-compassion, kindness, and even humor. The important thing here is to step out of the blame game all together. Ownership is beyond all of that. It's another game entirely—one that will continue to open doors to more satisfying choices, lifelong learning, insight, and empowerment.

If you are distressed by anything external, the pain is not due
to the thing itself but to your estimate of it; and this you have
the power to revoke at any moment.   **MARCUS AURELIUS**

10

THE NATURE OF CIRCUMSTANCES

L et's return our attention to the two different landscapes we
generated in the last chapter. In figure 10.1, you'll see the
word *Circumstances* written on the boundary that divides
the Empowerment Zone (taking ownership) from the Drama Zone
(assigning blame). If we can truly experience the same set of circumstances in these two remarkably different ways, it suggests that some
degree of choice is involved.

When we find ourselves in the Drama Zone with a victim narrative
running through our brain, feeling angry, upset, or hurt, we may not feel
as if we've made a choice. Nonetheless, if we've developed a pattern of
victim-thinking over the years, that in itself entails choices we've made
again and again, consciously or not. We might not always be able to recognize the choices as they arise in the moment, but the fact remains that
staying in the reactive-survival mode of the Drama Zone and stewing in
our own victimization is a choice, albeit a terrible one. Instead, we can
choose to find some way to own something—*anything*—that will get
us back to the responsive-relational mode of the Empowerment Zone.

This could simply mean owning our reactions with self-compassion and then choosing to respond in the best way possible.

PEOPLE ARE VICTIMIZED

I want to emphasize again that some people are truly victimized. Every day, people suffer unjust, heinous, cruel, and criminal forms of victimization. Any one of us can be struck down in the prime of life by debilitating accidents and illnesses. Innocent people are tragically victimized by war, ethnic cleansing, extreme poverty, structural violence, institutionalized racism, bigotry, and oppression. People are victimized by violent crimes as well as all kinds of fraud and property crimes. All of these tragedies and more are a sad and unfortunate part of the human experience.

I recognize that as someone living in a relatively prosperous and stable country, I enjoy tremendous advantages compared to millions of less fortunate people on our planet. I also realize that as an educated, white European-American male, I enjoy tremendous unearned privilege due to no other fact than my gender and the color of my skin. Some will argue that teaching others to move beyond blame, live in the Empowerment Zone, and follow the path of Radical Responsibility is in itself an expression of privilege. Others will even say that it's just another form of oppression exercised by those with more privilege against those with less. As a longtime social activist working for peace and justice, I'm very sensitive to these arguments; nonetheless, they would be missing the point.

I want to be very clear here: Radical Responsibility and the Empowerment Zone/Drama Zone distinction have absolutely nothing to do with blaming the victim. First of all, these distinctions in the Radical Responsibility model are not about others; they are for us. In following the path of Radical Responsibility, we don't wield these distinctions as weapons of judgment or criticism of others. That would,

> Radical Responsibility and the Empowerment Zone/ Drama Zone distinction are not in any way about blame.

THEMES		FEELINGS	
• Accountability	• I wasn't paying attention	• Challenge	• Learning
• Responsibility		• Confusion	• Understanding
• Ownership	• I didn't do my due diligence	• Empowerment	• Maturity
• I was: enabling colluding, rescuing, people-pleasing, distracted, unaware, lazy, conflict avoidant	• I could have seen it coming	• Less helpless	• Disorientation
	• I did see it coming	• Clarity	• Hopefulness
		• Calm	• Openness
	• I ignored that quiet voice within	• Peace	• Stability
		• Empathy	• Wisdom
		• Compassion	• Reasonableness
	• I didn't speak up	• Regret	• Capableness
• I had poor boundaries		• Embarrassment	• Resilience
	• I was in denial	• Relief	

Empowerment Zone
TAKING OWNERSHIP

Circumstances

Drama Zone
ASSIGNING BLAME

THEMES		FEELINGS	
• Injustice	• Deception	• Fear	• Shame
• Betrayal	• Incompetence	• Anger	• Guilt
• Abuse of power	• Unfairness	• Hurt	• Vengefulness
	• Unseen/not validated	• Confusion	• Sadness
• Exploitation		• Shock	• Powerlessness
• Misunder-standing	• Unfairly passed over	• Disbelief	• Hopelessness
		• Overwhelmed	• Despair
• Disrespect	• Bias, prejudice	• Frozen	• Anxiety
• Broken agreements	• Bigotry	• Rage	• Numbness
	• Racism	• Disappointment	• Isolation
• Violation of trust	• Politics		
	• Distrust		
• Dishonesty	• Oppression		

FIGURE 10.1 Ownership- and blame-based landscapes

in fact, be totally Drama Zone behavior. We also don't wield them as weapons against ourselves. Ownership equals choice and freedom, not self-blame.

In actuality, Radical Responsibility calls us to recognize with greater and greater clarity and subtlety all the ways in which we contribute to the victimization of others and all the ways in which we participate in harmful systems of oppression and ignorance, as well as all the ways in which we are not taking care of ourselves, each other, and all life on this planet. We do so not in order to blame ourselves, which again would land us squarely back in the Drama Zone, but rather to see clearly the causes of suffering and causes of happiness for ourselves and others, such that we can make more life-sustaining choices that are in the mutual best interests of all.

So when someone else is truly victimized, the last thing they need is for someone to tell them to get out of the Drama Zone. That would be a totally inappropriate and even violent thing to do. Instead, as I've said before, they most likely need their experience validated and affirmed before they can even begin their path of healing. We also have no idea what anyone's path of healing might or should look like. I think it's fair to say, though, that remaining trapped in a state of victimization will at the very least significantly limit their life possibilities. If we are significantly victimized in some way, the most responsible and self-empowering choice may be to seek validation for our victimization and the support we need for our healing. It may also include making boundaries and seeking justice. So just to be absolutely clear, Radical Responsibility and the Empowerment Zone/Drama Zone distinction are not in any way about blame. They're not about blaming others, and they're certainly not about blaming ourselves. We will continue to explore this critical distinction between Radical Responsibility and blame for the remainder of this book.

THE TRUE NATURE OF CIRCUMSTANCES

Returning to figure 10.1, notice again how the same set of circumstances can elicit insight and empowerment or drama and pain. The circumstances themselves are facts. We don't always agree on those facts, but for the sake of argument, let's just say that we have video footage of the event and that footage represents the circumstances. The events happened; they're in the past and they can't be changed. Do you see where I'm going with this? If it's possible for us to experience the very same set of circumstances in two utterly different ways (leading to two distinct experiences), then that implies a high degree of choice.

Of course, when we find ourselves in the Drama Zone and experience all the unfortunate feelings and storylines that go with that, we often don't feel as if we *chose* to land there. But even if that's the case and we simply find ourselves in the Drama Zone, we now have a choice whether or not to stay there. That choice is now our responsibility, and embracing it or not will determine our destiny.

Okay, so here comes the leap. If some degree of choice determines whether we experience a given set of circumstances in a *responsive-relational* (Empowerment Zone) or *reactive-survival* (Drama Zone) manner, it says something profound about the nature of the circumstances themselves. So please take a deep breath and contemplate the following idea:

Circumstances are neutral!

EXERCISE   Circumstances Are Neutral

Okay, I invite you to close your eyes for a moment, keep breathing, and repeat this phrase to yourself: "Circumstances are neutral, circumstances are neutral, circumstances are neutral." Hang in there and take a minute or two to reflect on the phrase and see what comes up for you. Just honor wherever that phrase takes you cognitively and emotionally. Whatever comes up, open your eyes after a couple of minutes and write down your thoughts and feelings in your Radical Responsibility journal.

Please don't skip over this exercise or shortchange yourself here. Doing the work and fully engaging the exercise is how you will learn about and transform your unconscious conditioning and belief systems—the secret programs that are running your life for better or worse!

For some of us, the phrase *circumstances are neutral* may feel liberating and empowering. It may even be exhilarating to consider that we, not circumstances, are in charge of our lives and destiny. On the other hand, we may find ourselves railing against such a preposterous notion. What do you mean that circumstances are neutral? How dare you! It could even come across as an outrageous, insensitive, and uncompassionate idea.

Regardless of what came up for you in the exercise above, I'm with you—some circumstances certainly don't feel neutral, and some are clearly horrific, unjust, and criminal. If that's the case, then what do I mean by "circumstances are neutral"?

To begin with, "circumstances are neutral" is not a value statement. It's not really even about circumstances themselves; it's about *us*. The statement itself is a distinction that points us in the direction of *choice*. In fact, the idea that circumstances are neutral is the key life distinction in the Radical Responsibility approach to life.

Life distinctions, as discussed in chapter 9, are meant to create leverage for change and transformation. To that end, they are intentionally radical, binary, and sharp-edged. Just as with the Empowerment Zone/Drama Zone distinction, there's no middle ground. We can't straddle the boundary. We have to land in one zone or the other when we realize that circumstances are neutral. The statement makes us focus, and that focus is solely placed on self-empowerment and choice. To quote Marcus Aurelius again, "Our destiny is not created by our circumstances but by our response to those circumstances."[1]

We aren't demonizing Drama Zone behaviors—they're just a part of being human.

THE DRAMA ZONE—FEAR-BASED, ADAPTIVE STRATEGIES FOR POWER AND CONTROL

Before thoroughly exploring how to shift to the responsive-relational mode (Empowerment Zone) and live there, we need to explore the

Drama Zone in detail. To begin with, I want to stress that we aren't demonizing Drama Zone behaviors—they're just part of being human. At the same time, with self-compassion and understanding we can begin to see that certain habituated and reactive behavior patterns are not serving us and can, in fact, be quite harmful.

We have a large number of fear- and survival-based Drama Zone strategies for dealing with feelings of powerlessness and uncertainty. They're all meant to help us regain some sense of power or control. Figure 10.2 shows four such strategies at the top of most of our lists.

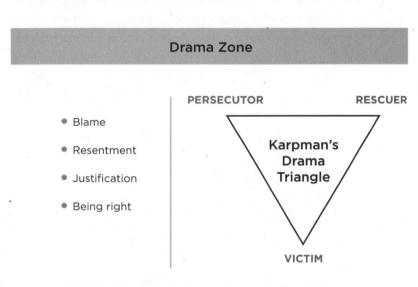

FIGURE 10.2 Classic Drama Zone adaptive strategies

Let's look at each of these in detail.

Blame
The minute most of us feel uncomfortable or unhappy about something, we almost instinctually look for an external cause. In doing so, we engage in *blame shifting*—blaming people or things outside of ourselves for our circumstances, thoughts, feelings, and behaviors,

rather than taking ownership for our experience. Why do we do this? Does it get us anywhere?

In my opinion, we do this because we have been conditioned into a culture and mindset of blame and shame to one degree or another. Most of us have been blamed for things from early on in our childhood and felt the accompanying sting of shame—the feeling of being rejected as unworthy and/or unlovable. We have been enculturated to believe that someone is always at fault and that if we don't manage to blame someone or something else, then the blame and shame will fall on us. So we naturally seek to protect ourselves and our tender hearts from further shame by blame shifting—finding someone or something to blame. Nonetheless, risky or not, ownership is the only place we have any genuine power. Self-compassion combined with the insight that blame shifting gives our power away will go a long way toward helping us choose freedom through Radical Responsibility.

I grew up in a family of five children. If my brother got into trouble, he would blame it on me. I would blame it on my older sister and she would blame it on our next sister, who would blame it on the youngest sister. The youngest sister didn't have another sibling to blame it on, so she would blame the dog. Most of us have experienced our share of blame and shame growing up, so we instinctually avoid it like the plague. When was the last time you heard a politician own up to something? Our entire political discourse in the United States these days consists almost entirely of the two main political parties blaming each other for not getting things done.

EXERCISE   Patterns of Blame Shifting

Open a new page in your Radical Responsibility journal and write "Patterns of Blame Shifting" at the top of a new page. Take a few deep breaths, connect with your innate basic goodness and the mind of self-compassion, and do your best to identify any habitual patterns of blaming others or circumstances when you are upset about something. Just keep writing until you have exhausted all the patterns of blame shifting you can identify.

> Remember, this is not about blaming ourselves. It is just about seeing clearly what is, so we can shift these disempowering (to ourselves) habitual patterns.

Resentment

Resentment—let's break this word down into its parts. *Re* indicates we are repeating something, doing it again and again. *Sent* is the Latin root of *sentire*, the word for feeling or sensing. *Ment* is a common suffix for nouns that denote a resultant state. So etymologically, *resentment* is the state that comes from repeating or recycling past emotions. Resentments are old feelings that we churn, rehash, build stories around, and often store as ammunition for future arguments.

Although we may not want to admit it, most of us have probably experienced resentment cycles in our relationships, former or current. We may have felt hurt or disrespected by the words or actions of our significant other, boss, coworker, or friend. Rather than finding a way to skillfully express our feelings, which would require courage and might lead to conflict, we stuff them into our resentment knapsack, where they fester and often leak out into our relationships as passive-aggressive behaviors or inappropriate humor. We may fantasize about creating a situation that would allow us to finally confront the other person, express our feelings, and right the wrong. Worse, we might indulge in revenge fantasies involving our perceived persecutor. Every time we fail to own our feelings or express them appropriately, we inadvertently convert them into resentments. In doing so, we saddle ourselves with the baggage of old feelings, and if that weren't bad enough, we also end up feeling inauthentic, which just leads to more resentment.

Of course, we don't need to express every feeling that comes up. However, we need to know the difference between genuinely letting something go—or appropriately seeking the best time and place to express our feelings or raise a concern—and stuffing our feelings into our knapsack of resentments. We fill this bag with all of our interpersonal bumps and bruises, and carry the increasingly heavy load wherever we go. Rather than owning our feelings and dealing with them in an empowering way, we just keep stuffing them in the sack. And we use the knapsack and its contents to validate our identification as a victim: "Look at all the terrible things that have happened to me! Look at all the ways I suffer! See what I have to deal with? I've been mistreated, and life is so unfair. Of course, I'm resentful!"

We can change the pattern and actually own our feelings and behaviors.

We may from time to time select a particularly juicy tidbit from our knapsack of smoldering feelings and slap someone with it (usually in the form of "always" or "never" statements—for example, "You never listen to me!"). And if we're feeling especially triggered, we might even hit someone over the head with the entire knapsack and its decades of resentments. Does this sound familiar? Most of us can probably relate to being on one side or the other of such a beatdown.

EXERCISE   Emptying Your Resentment Knapsack

Open a new page in your Radical Responsibility journal and write "Resentments" at the top. Okay, once more, take a few deep breaths, connect with the mind of self-compassion, and start writing down all the resentments you can think of that you have been stuffing away for as long as you can remember. Just keep writing until you have emptied your knapsack onto the pages of your journal. Once more, please keep in mind that this isn't about feeling bad about yourself—quite the opposite, in fact. This practice is all about freeing yourself from the burden of years of stored-up resentments.

Review your list of stored-up resentments and ask yourself this question: "Who's suffering?" This quote, attributed to Esther Lederer (a.k.a. Ann Landers), drives home the point: "Hanging onto resentment is letting someone you despise live rent-free in your head."[2] A similar teaching has been variously attributed to the Buddha, Nelson Mandela, Malachy McCourt, and Susan Cheever, among others: "Resentment is like taking poison and waiting for the other person to die."[3]

Justification

Rather than owning our behaviors and the impact they have on others, we justify and rationalize: "I had to," "She made me," "If only my boss hadn't . . ." and so on. Justification is another form of blaming. We blame our behaviors on someone or something else and make excuses to avoid responsibility, which is understandable, to some degree. We habitually act in these ways in order to protect ourselves from experiencing blame and shame.

Ownership is not another form of self-blame but a radical act of self-empowerment.

It doesn't have to be this way. We can change the pattern and actually own our feelings and behaviors. Embracing ownership and acknowledging self-agency regarding our feelings and behaviors is an act of radical self-empowerment, because the only place we have any real power is with ourselves. Justification—as well as blame, resentment, and the need to be right—undercuts that.

Look, managing our own feelings and behaviors isn't easy. It requires mindfulness, discipline, emotional intelligence, and commitment. We're up against the momentum of all the habitual patterns we've formed over our lifetime—everything mostly rooted in deeply imprinted childhood experiences. We're swimming upstream, so to speak, and the current is packed with fear-based neurobiological programming designed to keep us in a mechanical, reactive, and largely unconscious way of living. But we're strong swimmers! And with focused intention, commitment, and tenacity, we can actually free ourselves from these habitual patterns.

Being Right

Okay, here's the big one, the classic Drama Zone strategy. We love to be right, don't we? I know I do. Nothing feels more immediately satisfying than that deeply felt sense of *being right*. This one has a close cousin you might recognize: *I told you so!* Sound familiar?

Whatever form it takes, being right is the ultimate Drama Zone aphrodisiac. It gives us the strong internal affirmation of our rightness, and that's typically connected to deeply held victim identifications and righteous indignation. We get so attached to being right that we're willing to sacrifice our relationships. We get divorced over being right. Families break up over being right. Teams fail over being right. Partnerships and companies are destroyed over being right.

instances where you love to play the being right game (as well as the "I told you so" game). Just keep writing until you have found all these Drama Zone behaviors that you choose to stick with at the expense of your relationships. One last time: This is not an exercise in self-hatred. The point isn't self-criticism but finding our way back into self-empowerment and more genuine relationships through courageous insight.

All of these classic Drama Zone behaviors—blame, resentment, justification, and being right—arise from the fear- and survival-based victim mindset. They occur when we don't take ownership of our feelings and actions, fueled by the blame-and-shame paradigm that sadly dominates our culture. This paradigm comes with tragic consequences, but we aren't doomed to passively sit back and let it all simply happen to ourselves and others. As we have seen elsewhere, we can learn to let go of the instinct to blame and instead embrace ownership for our thoughts, feelings, and behaviors—and the consequences of those behaviors. Eventually, we come to understand that ownership is not another form of self-blame but a radical act of self-empowerment. We are actually capable of experiencing difficult emotions and owning them as feelings that arise from our perceptions of unmet or threatened needs, which in turn arise from the meaning we add to experiences based on our conditioning and, at best, limited interpretations of the available data. Within the Empowerment Zone landscape of owned perceptions and feelings, we can explore where we have a choice in how we perceive or think about a particular circumstance, as well as how we respond to it.

In some cases, you may be able to see your part in creating the circumstance in the first place. At the very least, you can own your freedom to choose how you perceive, understand, and respond to that circumstance. Even when you have already created new challenges for yourself by reacting unskillfully, you're able to stop, reflect, and see how you can respond—that is, not simply react—differently in the future. Owning your perceptions, feelings, and behaviors like this, as well as the consequences and impacts of your actions, in a blame-free context of self-compassion provides you access to the wisdom you need to make more informed, effective, and beneficial choices in the future. In doing so, you transition from a reactive mode of being to a responsive, creative, and mutually beneficial way of living in the world.

If you've done the exercises in this chapter (and those in the last chapter), I commend you for doing some truly difficult work. It can prove challenging and painful to explore the various ways we engage in *reactive-survival mode* (Drama Zone) thoughts and actions, but thankfully that's not the whole story. In the next chapter, we learn to make the shift to the responsive-relational mode (Empowerment Zone) and discover the world of limitless possibility and authentic relationship by embracing Radical Responsibility.

Just because you're an adult doesn't mean you're grown up. Growing up means being patient, holding your temper, cutting out the self-pity, and quitting with the righteous indignation. Why do so many people seem to love righteous indignation? Because if you can prove you're a victim, all rules are off. You can lash out at people. You don't have to be accountable for anything. **BRANDON STANTON**

11

DISCOVERING AUTHENTIC RELATIONSHIP

I n previous chapters we examined how we frequently operate in the reactive-survival mode (Drama Zone), employing fear-based, adaptive strategies to survive amid the challenges of modern life. Culturally, this Drama Zone context assumes that human nature is somehow inherently flawed and that—absent some form of shamed-based coercion—we will behave badly. Growing up in this shame-based culture, we internalize all kinds of limiting core beliefs about ourselves, others, and life all together, and these beliefs keep us trapped in cycles of fear-based adaptive behaviors.

The Drama Zone perspective is all about fear, survival, and constriction. We've become so accustomed to it though; it's like a straitjacket we don't even realize we're wearing. Our breath becomes shallow, our muscles and heart clench up, and our mind fills up with petty, discursive thoughts that keep us entertained and sedated. We become a distortion of our true selves—an unconscious character in our own Drama Zone reality TV show.

We've explored a number of strategies for waking up from the trance in order to transform the limiting core beliefs, adaptive strategies, and habitual behaviors that keep us trapped in the Drama Zone—the critical first stage of the journey. Now it's time to learn to live in the Empowerment Zone. It's time to step out of that straitjacket once and for all.

You now have permission to breathe properly, open your heart, and connect with the vastness and bravery of the unfettered heart-mind. You have permission to embrace your birthright to be here on this planet, to take up your square meter of space wherever you happen to be, to make appropriate use of available resources, and to thrive as a human being, free of any embarrassment whatsoever. Who gave you that permission? You did! By making it this far along the Radical Responsibility path and venturing into such new territory, you have empowered yourself to finally come home to yourself and claim your birthright as a human being.

You belong here. You are not a mistake. You can hold your head high and claim your freedom and dignity. So I invite you to continue the journey and shift your life context into the Empowerment Zone by embracing Radical Responsibility—radical ownership for your own life and destiny.

The Empowerment Zone is grounded in confidence in basic goodness—our own and that of others. Operating from this space, we open the door to genuine personal freedom, authentic relationships, and limitless possibility. The first key to shifting ourselves out of the Drama Zone is to realize the life distinction we discovered in the previous chapter: circumstances are neutral. Every time we remember that circumstances are neutral, we can then choose the best course of action to attain the results we want or need. In doing so, we place ourselves squarely back in the Empowerment Zone—the world of solutions and abundant options.

Now you're ready to take on the next important life distinction. This one will also play a key role in our ability to consistently shift and live in the responsive-relational mode (Empowerment Zone):

External Events or Other People's
Behaviors Do Not Cause Our Feelings

Conceptually, most of us already understand that. However, when it comes right down to it, most of us continue to blame other people or circumstances for our feelings. Here are some common ways we express this habit:

- You're pissing me off!

- You hurt my feelings.

- Of course, I'm angry. Who wouldn't be angry at that jerk?

- My boss humiliated me.

- This weather is so depressing . . .

Do any of these sound familiar? Of course, the assumption that other people and situations cause us to feel certain ways seems fairly compelling. Something happens, someone does or says something, and we immediately find ourselves feeling a certain way, for better or worse. The relationship between external events and our internal state appears and feels linear, direct, and causal. In truth, our emotions arise from our interpretation of external events and behaviors.

We saw in chapter 6 that feelings come up in response to our perception of whether or not our needs are being met, or whether they feel threatened in some way. When our needs are met, we feel good, experiencing positive emotions such as contentment, peacefulness, and joy. On the other hand, when we sense that our primary needs are threatened or that they won't be met, we experience challenging feelings such as sadness, disappointment, anxiety, irritation, anger, jealously, and envy.

We've also seen that our perceptions are not necessarily accurate assessments of what's actually happening. At best they're based on a limited or biased interpretation of a fairly narrow range of the available data. We continually add meaning to everything we experience within and around us, and the source of those interpretations lies in our childhood conditioning and other past experiences, which may or may not have any relevance to the present situation. Based on the meaning we add to our experiences, we make all kinds of assumptions and jump to conclusions. Indeed, there is a vast internal landscape situated between external events or other people's behaviors, and the feelings we almost automatically assume they cause.

This is not to say that there is anything wrong with our feelings. It's natural to feel sad or angry at times. The emotional part of our being is an important source of wisdom when consciously managed with awareness and healthy self-regulation. Nonetheless, it's helpful to realize that we have a lot more agency than we typically think regarding our emotions and how we relate to them. It's also beneficial to hold our perceptions and assumptions lightly, realizing what they're based on. And we can learn to check in with ourselves ("Hmm . . . What's really going on here? Have I jumped to conclusions?"). We can also explore different interpretations of any given situation. This, in turn, may lead us to feel differently and set us up for a more creative response to a particular circumstance.

The problem with being convinced that our feelings are caused by people and situations outside of ourselves is that we give away our power. We put other people and circumstances in charge of our own internal state and well-being. When we habitually do this, we depend more and more on events and people to change in order to feel differently. We have ceded all control to something over which we have little or no influence.

EXERCISE   Feelings and Needs

Let's explore this a little bit. Please open your Radical Responsibility journal to a new page and title it "Feelings and Needs." Then divide the page into three columns with the headings: "Feelings," "External Trigger," and "Unmet Need." Now begin thinking of situations in your daily life where you find yourself experiencing a challenging emotion such as anger, frustration, fear, jealousy, and so on, as well as where you usually attribute external causes for these particular feelings. In the far left column, write down the emotion or feeling. In the middle column, note the assumed cause or trigger. In the third column, put down the perceived unmet need underlying the emotion you experienced. Repeat this exercise with at least a half dozen situations, until you really get the distinction that feelings are not caused by external events but by our perception of met or unmet needs.

Based on these two related life distinctions—that is, circumstances are neutral, and external events or other people's behaviors do not cause our feelings—we can develop our capacity to live in the Empowerment

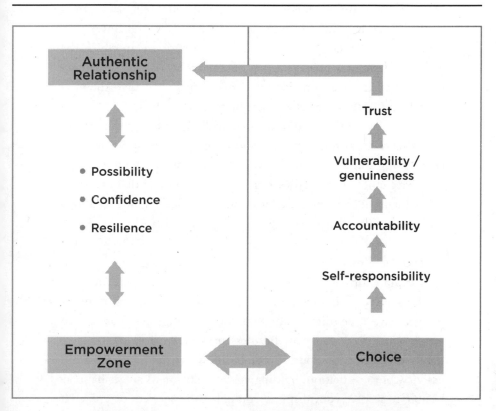

FIGURE 11.1 Steps for living in the Empowerment Zone

Zone, the domain of Authentic Relationship and limitless possibility, by practicing the three steps depicted below in figure 11.1 and explored in detail for the rest of this chapter. Please commit to engaging the exercises and take lots of notes. Don't skip ahead—this is where the rubber meets the road! This is where you actually learn to free yourself from the entanglements of *reactive-survival mode* drama, blame, and shame in order to live, work, and thrive in the Empowerment Zone.

STEP 1 RADICAL RESPONSIBILITY

At this point, I hope I've been able to convey that Radical Responsibility means to embrace 100 percent ownership for every circumstance we face in life, not as some kind of burden, self-sacrifice, or *should*, but as a radical act of self-empowerment. Once more, let me be absolutely clear: Radical Responsibility has absolutely nothing to do with blame. Responsibility and ownership do not equal self-blame. In fact, Radical Responsibility is grounded in a beyond-blame context—the context of our innate, unconditional basic goodness, in which there is no fundamental mistake. And because there is no fundamental mistake, we are free to make our personal mistakes, own them, and learn from those mistakes without blaming ourselves.

Some people might call that "being willing to accept the blame." I would say that is an unfortunate and misguided use of language with far-reaching consequences. The word *blame* comes with judgment and negative connotations, and we don't need any more of that in a culture where blame and shame are almost inexorably linked, one feeding the other in a toxic cycle.

Giving Our Power Away

Let's explore this idea of voluntarily claiming 100 percent responsibility for every circumstance we face. Let's say you and a business partner have a conflict. Something went wrong, and you are completely convinced that your business partner is to blame, that it is totally their fault. Of course, your business partner has quite a different view of the situation, holding you at fault for whatever happened. Unable to resolve your dispute, you enlist the services of a mediator, who patiently listens to both of your accounts of what happened. The mediator then reports that both of your stories are thoroughly convincing and that she is unable to discern who is at fault. However, it turns out that there is a videotape of what actually happened, so she suggests recruiting a focus group made up of intelligent, objective people who don't know either one of you and have no reason to favor either party.

You both agree with the plan. Eventually the mediator returns to report the results. She turns to you and says, "Well, the focus group did agree that what happened is more your business partner's fault than yours."

> We can't control other people and they can't control us.

"Thank you!" you respond triumphantly. "I'm so glad those people were smart enough to realize this is all my partner's fault!"

The mediator replies, "Well, to be precise, the focus group agreed that your partner bears about 60 percent of the responsibility, but you also bear some of the responsibility, about 40 percent."

Only partly believing it, you say, "Okay, I'll accept my 40 percent of the responsibility as long as we all agree this was mostly my partner's fault!" You feel vindicated; you won the argument.

But would it actually make sense to feel good about such an outcome? If you truly believe that your business partner is at least 60 percent of the cause of your upset and suffering, how much of your power did you just give away? If we believe something we are unhappy about is someone else's fault, are we not giving them power over our feelings and state of mind?

As it turns out, we can't control other people. So if I allow them to determine how I feel—much less what my possibilities are in life—I have just put them in charge of my feelings and, in some cases, my life. In doing so, what power do I have?

We can't control other people and they can't control us. Even when they try to do so, we usually find a way to do what we want. Take it from me: Even prisoners who are under constant supervision—even those in maximum security prisons—find ways to get their needs met. They enjoy smuggled food, cigarettes, alcohol, and drugs of all types. They get the guards to sneak things in for them, use mirrors to look around corners, and employ tapping signals on the bars to communicate with each other. One of the biggest challenges facing prison administrators these days is keeping cell phones out of prisons. Prisoners manage to get them smuggled in to stay in touch with family and friends, or in some cases use the phones to manage criminal enterprises on the outside. It seems that the more you try to control people, the more ingenious they become in resisting that control.

We regularly wish our spouses, children, parents, coworkers, friends, and strangers acted differently than they do. We waste so much energy agonizing about this—endlessly complaining about the behaviors of others, criticizing them behind their backs (or to their faces), seething with righteous indignation, and investing countless hours strategizing how to get them to do what we think they should do. All of this creates endless suffering for ourselves and others, but mostly for ourselves. Our efforts to control others are completely futile and simply a prescription for more pain and disappointment.

Unenforceable Rules

Fred Luskin, founder of the Stanford University Forgiveness Project, talks a lot about *unenforceable rules.*[1] Unenforceable rules are the unwritten expectations and demands we carry around regarding how other people are supposed to act. When anyone breaks one of our rules—which, if you're like me, happens all of the time—we find ourselves upset and angry, and we blame those feelings on the hapless person who broke one of our rules. These rules are unenforceable for the simple fact that we cannot control other people, no matter how reasonable our rules and expectations may seem to us.

You might have heard the axiom "Expectations are planned resentments." (I've heard my dear friend and mentor Roshi Joan Halifax say this many times, and the statement is also popular among the AA crowd.) It's okay to have wants and preferences, of course, but when we *expect* someone to follow our unenforceable rules, we're simply setting up ourselves and the unfortunate rulebreakers for more troubling feelings. It's difficult, but the more we learn to live and let live, the happier we will be.

Ironically, we rarely show the courtesy of sharing our rules with others, even those closest to us. However, it's probably a good idea to do so in our relationships (and it makes for a fun exercise). Let's try it out here.

EXERCISE   Unenforceable Rules

Start a new page in your Radical Responsibility journal with the heading "Unenforceable Rules." Pick a key person in your life, such as your partner, child, close friend, or boss. Without thinking too much about it, write down all the rules or expectations you have about how this person should behave. Just keep writing until you have completely exhausted all your rules. This exercise might take up several pages in your journal, but just keep writing. If you get stuck, think about anything that upsets you about this person's behavior. What do they do (or not do) that ticks you off?

How'd that go? Did you find this exercise enlightening? I certainly did. Here's my short list of rules for my girlfriend/partner:

- wake up every morning with a smile

- always be sweet, loving, and tender

- keep in shape and dress the way I like

- find me unbelievably hot and irresistible
  when I'm in the mood

- laugh at all my jokes

- appreciate my interest in politics and sports

- don't complain if I want to watch the news or sports on television

- listen to my stories with great interest

- don't interrupt me unless it's an emergency

- let me do my work in peace

- don't correct me in public .

- don't correct me in private

- provide me with sage advice and counsel, but only when I ask for it

- don't nag me about chores or items on the "honey do" list

- don't try to manage my behaviors (the pièce de résistance)

While I recognize the ridiculousness of this list, fortunately, for the sake of her sanity, as well as the harmony of our relationship, my sweetheart both breaks and keeps these rules on a regular basis. She got quite a kick out of this list when I shared it with her and actually added a couple I missed. We both had a good laugh!

Okay, enough about my list—what did you learn from yours? Does it help you see how you set yourself up for more suffering? I strongly encourage you to write down a list like this for every key person in your life. You could also make one for people in general—a master list that includes all of your pet peeves.

And if you haven't done the Unenforceable Rules exercise yet, please don't read on until you do. Just understanding the concept behind the exercise will not change anything. We need to do the work, and there is nothing more powerful than getting things down on paper and reflecting on what we have written.

Here's the next practice. Get ready—it takes a lot of imagination.

EXERCISE   Unhooked

Now take a few deep breaths and suspend disbelief for a second. Imagine not trying to control the people in your life anymore. Imagine how not trying to control others might, in fact, liberate you. Feel the freedom and ease of not having your state of mind and happiness depend on what others do or don't do.

Imagine if you could be happy despite your boss's narcissism, your coworker's repetitive stories, your partner's bad moods, your parents' constant advice, or your child's seeming entitlement. Try letting it all go. Just imagine that you are simply not hooked by the behaviors of the people around you. You see it all and you can appreciate the display with genuine interest, but you don't get hooked. It's not that you don't care—of course you care—but rather you have dropped your expectations about how it's supposed to be. You realize that people's behaviors are just expressions of their own needs, stories, dreams, and suffering, and it all ultimately has little or nothing to do with you.

After you've visualized this profound way of being for a few minutes, write down what you experienced. What might it tell you about what is possible?

STEP 2   ACCOUNTABILITY

Most of us have heard the expression "You are only as good as your word." Keeping our agreements is critical to our basic integrity; in leadership, there is no more important quality than integrity. Most of us break agreements with ourselves and others on a somewhat regular basis.

We make commitments knowing consciously or unconsciously that we are likely to break them, and we make all kinds of excuses for not keeping our word (if we even bother with an excuse): we were sick, the traffic was terrible, the car was acting up, the dog ate our homework, and so on.

All these excuses and lack of accountability undermines our integrity, as well as our confidence and feelings of self-worth. As human beings dealing with the complexities of modern life, we tend to avoid dealing with small breaches of our agreements and slip into patterns of unaccountability. Doing so creates more stress for us. We find ourselves living under a cloud of unmet agreements, fear of consequences, small lies, and cover-ups.

Let's say you have a report due that is several days late. You then find yourself engaging in all kinds of strategies to avoid a confrontation with your boss. You park blocks away from work; you avoid walking by their office. You bring your lunch and eat in your cubicle, in case your boss chooses to have lunch in the cafeteria. You head for the restroom when hearing your boss talking to a coworker nearby. Your nerves become frayed. You have nightmares about being fired. You start popping antacid tablets because your ulcer is acting up.

If you would simply take accountability and admit to yourself and your boss that you could not make the deadline, you would likely feel immediate relief from all the stress that your avoidance strategies end up creating. In all likelihood, you could, in good faith, renegotiate the report deadline and no longer have to sneak around the office. By reclaiming your dignity through accountability, you could park in your usual spot and enjoy your lunch without hiding. In essence, you would once again be free. By simply owning the situation as it is, you set yourself free from the self-imposed prison of unaccountability and avoidance.

We all know that dealing with our failings and challenges straightforwardly is the best course of action, but in the moment we find ourselves going the other way, avoiding accountability again and again. Something about our situation triggers unfortunate childhood memories of blame and shame, and we seek to escape by any means. As I relayed previously, my siblings and I quickly learned to blame each other to avoid punishment. How often do we see political leaders follow the "deny until you die" strategy when accused of wrongdo-ing, only to suffer further shame and harsher consequences when finally held accountable by the sure weight of the evidence? It is painfully ironic that we so fear accountability, when it is actually the royal road to personal freedom, success, and happiness, to say nothing of personal, professional, and spiritual growth and evolution.

Trust creates relationship.

STEP 3 VULNERABILITY—BEING REAL AND GENUINE

Vulnerability is the birthplace of love, belonging, joy, courage, empathy, and creativity. It is the source of hope, empathy, accountability, and authenticity. If we want greater clarity in our purpose or deeper and more meaningful spiritual lives, vulnerability is the path. **BRENÉ BROWN**

Vulnerability often gets a bad rap. For many, the word connotes weakness and exposure. In contrast, what I'm talking about here is more in line with research professor and best-selling author Brené Brown's message above. Vulnerability simply means being open-hearted, real, and honest with ourselves and others. It means not being afraid to be who we really are; and even when afraid, finding the courage to be ourselves anyway. Chögyam Trungpa Rinpoche describes such a person as a *warrior*, someone willing to acknowledge their own confusion and suffering.[2] In other words, a warrior is willing to be vulnerable, to feel and be seen—not hiding from oneself or others; not running away, shutting down, or acting out. Instead, as we first discussed in chapter 2, we can *hold our seat* in the midst of our shakiness and tenderness and stay with the rawness of our experience.

Authentic Relationship

Okay, so imagine that you and I have a personal or professional relationship of some kind and that I basically own my own thoughts and feelings and don't blame my problems on you. Furthermore, imagine that I keep my agreements with you—I do what I say I'm going to do, and I'm willing to be accountable. Now imagine that I'm also willing to be vulnerable, real, and genuine with you. All of that creates trust—true trust—and trust creates relationship.

I call the Empowerment Zone the domain of *Authentic Relationship*. This book is all about realizing our highest potential, and that's not something we can do in isolation. We are social beings; we need each other. And we can only reach our highest potential when in relationship with others aspiring to do the same. If we want a rewarding life, a key place to focus is the quality of our relationships.

Of course, most of our Drama Zone behaviors involve relationships too. There's no shortage of Drama Zone buddies who will endlessly play out dramas with us. However, these fear- and shame-based relationships are not our focus on the path of Radical Responsibility. Instead, we focus on Empowerment Zone relationships built on Radical Responsibility, accountability, vulnerability-genuineness, and trust.

EXERCISE   Authentic Relationships

Part 1   Please start a new page in your Radical Responsibility journal titled "Authentic Relationship" and write down the five most authentic relationships you have with people in your life. Once you have named them, go through each one and write down in some detail the characteristics that make it an authentic relationship. This could be a bulleted list of Empowerment Zone qualities that you consistently bring to that relationship.

When that feels complete, go back through all five relationships and write down ways in which you are, at times, still in the Drama Zone in those relationships. You can also note ways that you could bring even more authenticity to those relationships and, in the process, create more value and possibility for yourself and the other person. Do this as honestly and thoroughly as you can. Be sure to focus on your contributions to the relationship, not the other person's behaviors. This practice is about owning your part in creating the highest potential in any relationship.

Once you have competed your work, develop a gradual plan for improving each of these relationships by exercising even greater Radical Responsibility, accountability, and vulnerability-genuineness. Having made your plan, commit to it. And if you really want to be brave, share your work with the other person (if you feel like they can receive it well).

Part 2 This is the tough part. Muster your courage, self-compassion, and confidence in your own unconditional goodness. Now write down the names of the five people with whom you have significant personal or professional relationships where you most often find yourself in the reactive-survival mode (Drama Zone). Under each of those names, list all the ways in which your participation in that relationship creates drama—ways in which you blame, project, don't own your feelings, aren't accountable, break agreements, tell lies, don't keep clear boundaries, avoid difficult conversations, hold back, shut down, participate in drama, and so on. See if you can identify where you are caught in Drama Triangles and what roles you play in those.

Breathe deeply. Remember that all of this is nothing but old tapes running where you have yet to commit to mindfulness and staying in the Empowerment Zone. With self-compassion, develop a plan for making steady, incremental improvements in these relationships. In some cases, this may mean having better boundaries or disengaging from a relationship entirely, but you can do so by owning your part, keeping your heart open, and wishing the other person all the best in their life journey. For those relationships in which it makes sense to continue, create a gradual plan for bettering them through owning your part in any dramas and committing yourself anew to Radical Responsibility, accountability, and vulnerability-genuineness to the best of your ability. Having made your plan, commit to it. Again, if you feel up to it, share your plan with the people in those relationships. You might be amazed to find that they too long for healthier and more authentic relationships with you.

To summarize, when met with discomfort, our tendency is to attribute the cause of our unease to someone or something outside of ourselves. In doing so, we disown our agency and personal power. We ignore the entire inner landscape of our conditioning, interpretations, and assumptions. We externalize our unwanted experience by making projections, shifting the blame, and instinctually embracing a victim mindset. This effort to protect our tender heart is quite natural, so we need to observe it with a healthy dose of self-compassion. At the same time, we need to honestly face the destructive impact of the victim mindset and any tendency we might have to give away our power.

Again, I invite you to consider that no matter how hard we try, we simply can't control others. The crux of this book lies in accepting that fact. Radical Responsibility requires keeping the focus on ourselves and directing our own behaviors toward the results we aspire to achieve in life. In case you're wondering, this does not mean being a doormat for others—far from it. Part of being responsible is maintaining good boundaries and negotiating clear agreements with others. We can do this by clearly recognizing our own and others' agency, as well as holding ourselves responsible for the results we create through our own decisions and behaviors. In the Empowerment Zone domain of Authentic Relationship, there is no limit to the good we can achieve.

Our deepest fear is not that we are inadequate. Our deepest fear is that we are powerful beyond measure. It is our light, not our darkness that most frightens us. We ask ourselves, "Who am I to be brilliant, gorgeous, talented, fabulous?" Actually, who are you not to be? . . . Your playing small does not serve the world. There is nothing enlightened about shrinking so that other people won't feel insecure around you. We are all meant to shine, as children do. . . . As we are liberated from our own fear, our presence automatically liberates others. **MARIANNE WILLIAMSON**

12

THE EMPOWERMENT TRIANGLE AND RADICAL POSSIBILITY

In chapter 5 we explored Stephen Karpman's Drama Triangle in depth and saw how this incredibly destructive dynamic will play out in our individual and collective lives until we awaken to the greater power of our innate basic goodness. The human condition unexamined is a prescription for servitude to the fear-based survival instinct, genetically hardwired into our brain for good reason but that, unchecked, creates the ocean of human suffering. This very same human condition, consciously owned and examined to its depths, becomes instead the vehicle for realizing our highest human potential.

We also learned strategies in chapter 6 for getting off the Drama Triangle and avoiding a great deal of unnecessary relational toxicity and suffering. Unfortunately, the victim, persecutor, and rescuer roles—as well as the adverse triangulation they entail—are deeply embedded in our individual psyches and the culture we share. It's no accident that this archetypal dynamic is the basic narrative structure for our favorite novels and television dramas.

So what if we could actually transform the Drama Triangle? What if we could transmute that Drama Zone vortex of negativity and suffering into a different kind of triangle? As the title of this chapter indicates, we're about to examine how to create an Empowerment Zone triangle (see figure 12.1)—one that promotes positivity, possibility, creative solutions, and the very best of our human potential.

The Empowerment Triangle looks a little bit like an inverted Drama Triangle, but you won't find the victim, persecutor, or rescuer roles represented there. They simply don't belong to the contexts of the Empowerment Zone and Authentic Relationship. As we saw earlier, these roles are all based in victim mentality—they arise in reaction to feelings of powerlessness, woundedness, and a lack of control. So our first challenge in establishing the Empowerment Triangle is to transform these fear-based adaptive strategies into a more empowering archetype.

What can I do?

Before going further, I want to give a nod to my colleague David Emerald and his brilliant book *The Power of TED* (*The Empowerment Dynamic)*, which presents something quite similar to the material you'll find here.[1] David and I had the opportunity to share our work together in 2007, and the similarities (and differences) in our models will be apparent to anyone familiar with both. I strongly recommend David's work, and I particularly appreciate his powerful use of allegory.

TRANSFORMING THE VICTIM MINDSET

When facing a challenging circumstance—whether we feel we had anything to do with creating it or not—how can we shift from feeling helpless to feeling empowered? Rather than feeling trapped by circumstances, getting lost in blame, and sinking further into the quicksand of the victim mindset (and jumping right back on the Drama Triangle), we want to shift our focus to a sense of freedom, empowerment, and possibility. The key life distinction I presented in chapter 10—that is, circumstances are neutral—offers a new perspective in the face of challenging or difficult events (and people). From this fresh vantage point, we no longer react to unwanted circumstances with the classic *reactive-survival mode* (Drama Zone) question Why me? but instead meet them with a *responsive-relational mode* (Empowerment Zone) response: What can I do?

This powerful question is the gateway to the Empowerment Zone domain of limitless possibility. The moment we ask ourselves, What can I do? we are no longer trapped in the victim mindset and the

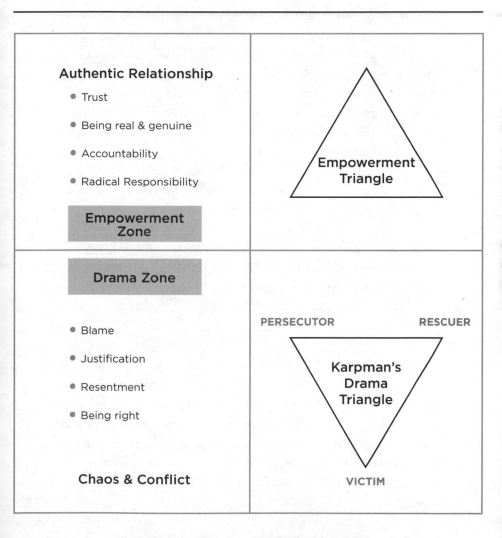

FIGURE 12.1 Transforming the Drama Triangle

fear-driven world of limitations. This magical question launches us into the world of solution-based thinking, creativity, and innovation. What can I do? immediately opens the door to what I call the *co-creative mind*, or the *co-creator* archetype positioned at the apex of the Empowerment Triangle (see figure 12.2).

EXERCISE   Discovering the Co-Creator

Okay, grab your Radial Responsibility journal and write "The Co-Creator" at the top of a blank page. Think of an uncomfortable situation you are struggling with and write down a short phrase explaining the situation that will help you recognize it later. Now, keeping that situation in mind, ask yourself, *What can I do?* Watch what arises. Can you feel yourself shifting away from a victim mindset and into a co-creative one? Can you sense possibilities and solutions arising?

If you still feel stuck, keep going. Hold the situation in mind and just keep asking yourself, What can I do? Write down your reflections and any new possibilities or solutions that emerge. You may want to try this with several situations to really ground yourself in this new experience. I encourage you to practice repeating this question—What can I do?—anytime you find yourself stuck and struggling with something.

From the perspective of the co-creative mind, we continually ask ourselves, "What is the most creative, empowering, and beneficial way for me to respond to any given circumstance?" Instead of being reactive or passive, this empowering response immediately provides us access to the realm of possibility by placing our attention on solutions and alternatives, as opposed to problems and limitations. It grounds us firmly in the realm of *choice*, where we reclaim our power to *choose*.

From *You* to *I*; from Blame to Ownership

Here's how it works: When we find ourselves getting caught in the victim mindset and Drama Zone behaviors such as blaming our discomfort and pain on someone or something outside ourselves, we simply shift the language and assume ownership, at least for our feelings. Instead of engaging in the projective *You* language of blame, we switch to the reflective *I* language of ownership—for example, "I'm angry," "I'm upset," "I'm afraid."

This seemingly simple substitution can move mountains. In the victim position, we focus entirely on the other person and give them power over us.

In the ownership or co-creative mind position, we focus on ourselves and the actions that will reclaim our power. When we don't make others responsible for our feelings and circumstances, we empower ourselves to take charge of our own destiny. We own the feelings (for example, "I'm upset") as well as the circumstance ("Somehow I'm in this position where I'm not getting my needs met"), and we ask ourselves empowering questions ("What can I do to shift this?").

It can be helpful to see how we may have contributed to getting into the unfavorable circumstance in the first place—not to blame ourselves but simply for the purpose of learning how to take a different

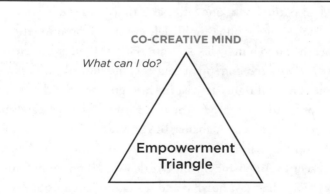

FIGURE 12.2

The co-creative mind at the apex of the Empowerment Triangle approach in the future. However, even if we can't see that we had anything to do with it, we can still own our power to choose the most creative and beneficial response.

Of course, this is often much easier said than done. Life happens. We can't control the world—bad, unjust, and horrific things happen. However, we know that people who have had to contend with horrendous circumstances—people genuinely victimized by abuse, violence, catastrophic illness, and all forms of oppression—have found ways to eventually transform their victimization by becoming survivors. In some cases, they even become transformers, inspiring others who've been victimized in similar ways to not only survive but thrive.

Several examples come to mind of people who faced severe physical or mental disabilities but chose to be survivors rather than victims, and they went on to become powerful role models for others. Ray Charles and Stevie Wonder were both legally blind but produced bodies of work that changed popular music forever. Theoretical physicist Stephen Hawking, completely paralyzed by amyotrophic lateral sclerosis, became renowned for his groundbreaking scientific contributions to astrophysics and cosmology, in particular, his work on black holes. Helen Keller—blind and deaf from an early age—went on to become a famous author, political activist, and lecturer who drew on her challenges to inspire millions. When French author Jean-Dominique Bauby suffered a stroke that left him completely paralyzed, he dictated an entire book, one letter at a time, to his editorial assistant, communicating by blinking his left eye in response to letters of the alphabet shown to him by his assistant. He wrote an entire memoir, *The Diving Bell and the Butterfly*, using this method. Rosa Parks, an African American civil rights activist in the segregated South, defied a bus driver's order to give up her seat to a white passenger, catalyzing the successful Montgomery, Alabama, bus boycott—a pivotal moment in the history of the civil rights movement. Viktor Frankl, the Austrian psychiatrist sent to Auschwitz during World War II, not only found a way to survive in the most horrific and degrading circumstances one can imagine, but went on to reach countless people with his book *Man's Search for Meaning* and his psychotherapeutic model, logotherapy. It's telling that one of Frankl's principal discoveries during his time in the Auschwitz slave labor camp was that, no matter how dire, horrific, and powerless our circumstances may be, we still have a choice that no one can take from us—we can choose the attitude we bring to those circumstances.

These people had to face more extreme challenges than most of us ever will. They demonstrate that no matter how bad things get, we can still find some way to access the co-creative mind and our power to choose how best to respond to any circumstance. Many of us regularly fall into victim mindsets and get caught on the Drama Triangle in relation to fairly minor life challenges. We don't have to feel bad about that—it's simply how we've been conditioned. Life is challenging for all of us, and it takes both tremendous courage and a substantial dose of self-compassion to keep our heads up and our hearts open throughout it all. However, since you've made it this far into the book, you can no longer claim ignorance or abdicate your responsibility to overcome the conditioning that no longer serves you. This realization and choosing to get into the driver's seat of your own life open up a vast panorama of exciting possibilities.

It may be shocking to realize at this point that we are actually the author of much of our own suffering, and that we may even be hanging on to this suffering because it meets our needs for identity and significance. This can be a daunting discovery that could easily send us spiraling down into the black hole of self-blame and shame. Instead, we can see our challenges as part of the human journey and commit ourselves to learning how to transcend our fear-based approaches to life with bravery and compassion.

> There is nobody to blame. There is no ultimate mistake—things are as they are.

Radical Responsibility and the Empowerment Triangle are about stepping out of the paradigm of blame all together. There is nobody to blame. There is no ultimate mistake—things are as they are. From the perspective of the co-creative mind, we're free from the weight of blaming ourselves and others and can work with our present circumstances with tremendous energy and creativity. Realizing that we are all in this together naturally extends and fuels our compassion for others. We can envision a better world for all of us, co-created through collective responsibility, bravery, and kindness.

If we aspire to change our outlook, rewire our brains, and devote ourselves to habits that better serve us, we first need to develop an experiential confidence in our unconditional *basic goodness*. Mindfulness meditation (as presented in chapter 2) naturally encourages a more accepting and compassionate stance toward ourselves and our moment-to-moment experience. Through mindfulness practice, we develop stabilized attention, mental clarity, and emotional balance, as well as an open, curious, and more equanimous relationship to ourselves and whatever arises in our field of attention. Furthermore, mindfulness allows us to experience what Buddhists call *maitri* in Sanskrit and *metta* in Pali, often translated as "unconditional friendliness" or "loving-kindness."

I'll present specific practices for developing maitri, self-compassion, and resilience in the next chapter. For now, I invite you to try an exercise designed to lessen the impact of fear-based conditioning and increase your resilience—a practice that encourages you to let go of the past and rewire your brain. You can do it at any time, in any place of your choosing. You can try it for just a couple of minutes or for as long as you like.

◀)) **EXERCISE**   **Safe, Resourced, and Connected**[2]

Sitting in a chair, standing, or lying down, find a posture that feels naturally uplifted, relaxed, and stable. Gently get in touch with your body as it is right now. Feeling the physical sensations at the point of contact between your body and the chair, your feet and the ground, gently anchor your attention in the moment-to-moment felt presence of your body. If your attention wanders into discursive thinking or other distractions, gently bring it back to feeling the physical sensations of your body, and do your best to recommit to being present.

In this exercise, we're going to gradually retrain our mind to operate with less anxiety and more regularly contact a sense of well-being. In doing so, we're not checking out or ignoring the fact that we often meet challenging situations in life. Our focus instead is on recognizing that much of the time, things are actually more or less okay, and we could notice and appreciate that fact so that our brain is not overloaded with fear all the time. To that end, it's best to do this practice at a time and in a place where you can feel relatively safe and resourced.

Safe (two minutes)   First, contemplate the fact that right here, right now, in this moment, you are safe. Perhaps you have memories of feeling unsafe, and you likely will experience difficult situations in the future. However, right here and now, you are safe, in a secure environment and relatively free from danger. Just keep contemplating this and feel the quality of being safe in your body and mind. Keep repeating the following phrase and reflect on the safety of your present situation: "Right here, right now, I am safe and free from danger."

Resourced (two minutes)   Now contemplate the fact that your basic needs for food, warmth, shelter, water, and so on, are currently being met. Though you may have concerns about the future or memories of feeling unresourced in the past, just keep returning to the fact that right here, right now, you are resourced and your needs are met. Feel the quality of being resourced in your body and mind. Keep repeating that phrase and reflecting on the resourced quality of your present situation for the next few minutes: "Right here, right now, my basic needs are met, I am resourced."

Connected (two minutes)   Now contemplate the fact that you are connected with other people, that you are not alone. Bring to mind the positive relationships you have with family members, friends, coworkers, and the like. You may feel lonely at times—that's part of life—but right here, right now, you could take in and appreciate the fact that you are connected to other beings, that you are not alone. Feel the quality of this connection in your body, heart, and mind. Keep repeating the following phrase and reflect on the connected quality of your present situation for the next few minutes: "Right here, right now, I am connected to other human beings, I have people and supportive relationships in my life."

Rest (one minute)   Finally, simply rest with confidence in these realities of your present situation—in this moment and in this place, you are safe, resourced, and connected. Allowing your breath to relax into its own natural rhythm, simply breathe the visceral feelings of being safe, resourced, and connected into your nervous system, your heart, and your bones.

TRANSFORMING THE PERSECUTOR

The persecutor mindset—controlling, criticizing, and dominating—seems fairly irredeemable. There's an old saying in India that if you truly want to achieve enlightenment, get yourself a Bengali teaboy. Evidently, Bengali teaboys are renowned (fairly or not) for being rather irritating and cantankerous; traditional literature is full of tales of teaboys provoking and tormenting whoever they're serving.[3] On the Drama Triangle, a Bengali teaboy is a classic persecutor. However, for spiritual practitioners devoted to enlightenment, such a figure acts much like the irritating grain of sand in the oyster that eventually creates an exquisite pearl. In other words, there's a lot more to the persecutor role than initially meets the eye.

Maybe there's that person at work who always points out what's wrong or missing. It might pain us to admit it, but they're often right—it's just that they're annoying or overly aggressive about it. Such a person rocks the boat; they constantly challenge us. And just like the Bengali teaboy, they prompt us to wake up and rise to the occasion. Most of the time when we're confronted with someone we view as a persecutor, we hop right on the Drama Triangle in the victim role; if their persecuting energy is directed elsewhere, we hop on as the rescuer. There's another way to respond, however. We can view the persecuting person or situation as a challenge and an opportunity for growth.

In a similar vein, Carlos Castaneda writes of "petty tyrants." In the Toltec tradition of Castaneda's shaman-mentor, the best possible thing that could happen to someone on their quest for liberation would be to encounter a petty tyrant. According to Castaneda, "A petty tyrant is a tormentor. Someone who either holds the power of life and death over warriors or simply annoys them to distraction."[4] When confronted with petty tyrants, we can either fall into the victim mindset or meet the challenge by rising to a higher state of mastery. The key, according to Castaneda, is to not take ourselves too seriously and the affronts of petty tyrants personally. We can choose to view our persecutors in a different light. Because they provoke us and shake us out of our comfort zone, they can actually become some of our most profound teachers.

As figure 12.3 shows, on the Empowerment Triangle, we call the transformed persecutor the *challenger*. Challengers reflect the world back to us, providing us with opportunities to see what needs to be shifted. Without the energy of the challenger archetype, we become complacent; for organizations, this typically means losing the creative and competitive edge. We all need challengers in our lives so we don't just go to sleep, captivated by the trance of the familiar.

> We all need challengers in our lives so we don't just go to sleep, captivated by the trance of the familiar.

Not only is it important to courageously and skillfully embrace the challengers who show up in our lives, but it is also necessary that we learn to become effective challengers ourselves without becoming persecutors. Can we learn to challenge our coworkers, bosses, family members, friends, and ourselves without persecuting and somehow making them or ourselves feel bad or wrong? This rare, high-level skill is much needed in our world. Truly effective challengers are in great demand. Learning how to be one without that persecuting energy will all but guarantee you an interesting life and livelihood. Highly paid business consultants and executive coaches have mastered this art. My intent with this book and the path of Radical Responsibility is to introduce you to the challenger archetype in a manner that you will find empowering and inspiring rather than demeaning.

EXERCISE   **Discovering the Challenger**

Okay, please open your Radical Responsibility journal to a new page and title it "The Challenger." To begin with, start writing down examples of ways in which you feel you are effective at challenging yourself and others without persecuting or making yourself or others feel wrong. Take the time to reflect on and appreciate your strengths in this regard.

Now think of those situations in which, out of a desire to create change, you tend to persecute yourself or others. After you have named as many situations as you can, reflect on how you might challenge yourself or others in those same situations without persecuting.

This is an important step, so don't skip it. Developing your skills as an effective challenger will set you apart and allow you to make significant contributions not only to your own progress, but also to the betterment of any family dynamic, team, or organization of which you are a part. If you are a parent, being able to skillfully challenge your adolescent children in a way they can receive it is pure gold!

Next, please write down as many situations that come to mind in which you feel persecuted by the behaviors of others at work or at home, especially those where the persecuting feels chronic to you—for example, the actions of a tyrannical boss. Now reflect on how you could take this situation as a challenge and use it to develop your emotional intelligence skills. Here's a wonderful opportunity to revisit the *What can I do?* question. Write down all your insights and especially any new ideas you have for creatively dealing with these challenging situations.

Finally, take a moment to reflect on anyone in your life who has been an expert challenger. Write down their name

---

and any details that describe what makes them such a helpful challenger for you and others.

TRANSFORMING THE RESCUER

As you'll recall from chapter 5, some rescuers are perfectly fine as they are. For example, professional and volunteer rescue teams provide an amazing service to all of us, and thankfully people continue to devote themselves to these and similar professions. That's not the type of rescuer we want to transform here.

Instead, we want to focus on those rescuers whose identity and ego needs are wrapped up in psychologically, emotionally, or physically rescuing other people. This type of rescuer has several different faces and names—*expert*, *fixer*, or *savior*, for example. In terms of the destructive *reactive-survival mode* dynamics of the Drama Triangle, the white hat-wearing rescuer is just as involved in perpetuating the drama as the black hat-wearing persecutor.

Now remember, we're talking about a mindset or archetype here, not actual people. Hardly anyone is a pure rescuer, and most of us in the helping professions have at least some ego investment in being helpers. Hopefully we're primarily motivated by genuinely altruistic intentions

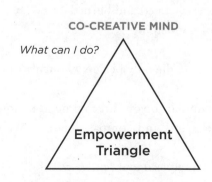

CO-CREATIVE MIND

What can I do?

Empowerment
Triangle

CHALLENGER

FIGURE 12.3 The challenger position of the Empowerment Triangle

and compassion, but it is admittedly a mixed bag for most of us. Ideally we become curious about this dynamic and willing to separate the healthy aspects of our motivation to be helpful from our egoic need to be in the rescuer position. In particular, we want to become aware of any ways in which our helping actually disempowers, disrespects, or demeans others. As I touched on in chapter 5, there are some telltale signs that we're caught up in the rescuer mindset on the Drama Triangle:

- We find ourselves getting involved in lots of drama.

- We habitually try to fix other people
  or change them for the better.

- We regularly feel resentful that people don't appreciate us.

- We tend to be the person everyone comes to
  with their victim stories and complaints.

- We're convinced that if we don't show up for
  work, the whole place will fall apart.

- We find ourselves feeling resentful about
  all the time we give to others.

- We become overwhelmed and burned
  out from all of our helping.

- We feel as if we are the only person who truly cares.

If any of these feel familiar to you, I recommend taking a closer look at your rescuing behaviors and compassionately investigating what drives them.

But what's the alternative? How can we transform the rescuer and actually help others in ways that empower them? We want to support people not by standing above them but beside them—eye to eye in a position of equality and mutuality. When others need help, we shouldn't view them as broken, but as whole and full of potential, just like us. Some words that describe this *responsive-relational* (Empowerment Zone) way of supporting people are *friend, ally,* and *mentor,* but I prefer the word *coach.*

Coaches provide training, support, cheerleading, and effective feedback, but they remain on the sidelines and let the players experience their own victories and defeats. They respectfully let people play out the game, address their own challenges, and live their own lives. Good coaches see the potential in others and help them see and realize it in themselves. Their reward comes from watching others grow and thrive, not from having others become dependent on them or see them as saviors or fixers. Coaches don't get out there and play the game for us, but they inspire and train us. They teach us how to solve problems. They mentor and encourage us.

EXERCISE   Actualizing the Coach

Please start a new page in your Radical Responsibility journal and write "The Coach" at the top. First, write down all the ways in which you do a skillful job coaching yourself and others. Make sure this list is free of rescuing behaviors. Take time to reflect on and appreciate your existing strengths in this regard.

Next, after connecting with your basic goodness and practicing self-compassion, reflect on as many situations as you can think of where you tend to get caught in the rescuer position. Just write down short phrases that capture these examples. After completing this list, reflect on how you might shift into a coach mindset in order to approach similar situations differently in the future. It may also be helpful to reflect on great coaches you have worked with—people who have supported you without enabling or disempowering you. Write down their names and some details about their qualities and habits.

When I was a hospice volunteer in prison, I came across a particular phrase from a nursing journal that I use to this day: *coming alongside*. The researcher used this nautical expression to describe her vision of ideal hospice care. For this nurse-author, coming alongside someone who is ill or dying means to simply and respectfully accompany them on their journey for a time. It means to bear witness to their stories, sufferings, and joys, and to support them as needed or requested, but with complete respect for their personhood, without any sense of fixing whatsoever. As a longtime sailor, I love this analogy for supporting others from the context of the Empowerment Zone, and I try my best to embody this approach with my coaching and consulting clients.

Take a look at the Empowerment Triangle now. The Drama Triangle roles of victim, persecutor, and rescuer have all taken new *responsive-relational mode* forms in the Empowerment Zone.

You'll also see that each transformed role comes with a corresponding slogan. For the co-creator, it's I can do it! (or, for a team, We can

Authentic Relationship

CO-CREATIVE MIND

What can I do?   I can do it!

Empowerment Triangle

Just do it!   You can do it!

CHALLENGER   COACH

FIGURE 12.4

The Empowerment Triangle—co-creative mind, challenger, and coach

do it!). For the challenger, it's Just do it! And the coach emphatically says, "You can do it!"

My first meditation teacher, Chögyam Trungpa Rinpoche, spoke to us this way—with love and conviction—all of the time. (He especially liked to say "You can do it!" and "Just do it!") He was the consummate challenger-coach, and he lived his life completely from the co-creative mind, positively influencing me and many thousands more during his lifetime and to this very day—many years since his passing in 1987. The same could be said of many other influential leaders and spiritual figures who have left lasting positive legacies. Upon examining their lives, you would likely find that they lived in the Empowerment Zone, at least to some degree, and embodied the context and skills of the Empowerment Triangle. By the way, this does not require perfection—neither from our role models or us. The most inspiring leaders throughout history have all had their challenges just like the rest of us. However, in finding ways to shift to the responsive-relational mode of the Empowerment Zone again and again, they were able to lead and influence others through some form of Radical Responsibility.

In figure 12.5 on the next page, you can now see the complete Radical Responsibility model. The Drama Zone is defined by fear, limitations, problems, and anxiety. This is the home of the Drama Triangle and the victim, persecutor, and rescuer archetypes, as well as the classic Drama Zone adaptive strategies of blame, resentment, justification, and insistence on being right.

The Empowerment Zone world of Authentic Relationship is characterized by possibility and solutions, fearlessness and bravery, and confidence in our intrinsic goodness, wholeness, and resilience. We access this domain by embracing Radical Responsibility, accountability, and vulnerability-genuineness, which together create trust—the ground of Authentic Relationship. And finally, as we just examined, in the Empowerment Zone we have the Empowerment Triangle, where we embrace the archetypes and skills of the co-creator, challenger, and coach.

By now I hope it's clear how tragically destructive being on the Drama Triangle can be:

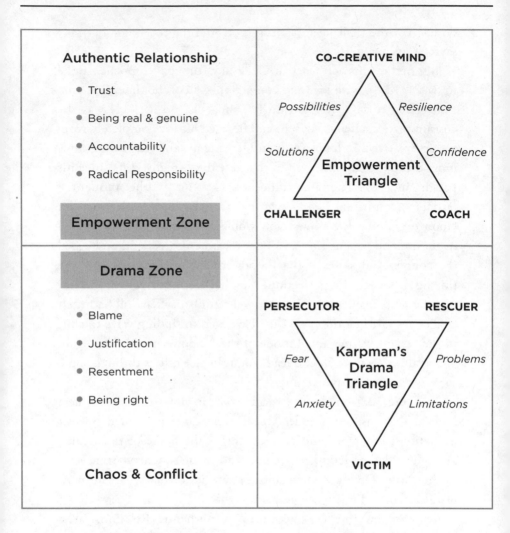

FIGURE 12.5   The complete Radical Responsibility model

- Individually, it undermines our efforts to realize our authentic purpose and manifest our true destiny.

- With others we're close to—for example, our partners and family members—it promotes conflict of all sorts, even neglect, abuse, and violence.

- At the community level, manifestations of the Drama Triangle include racism, hate crimes, police brutality, poverty, and overall degradation of society.

- Finally, at the global level, the Drama Triangle dynamic plays out endlessly as war, genocide, ethnic cleansing, refugee crises, and environmental disasters of all sorts.

The common thread running through all of these terrible manifestations of the Drama Triangle—as well as the reason for this summary review—is avoidance of responsibility. All of this (and sadly more) can occur when we give away our power and decline to take responsibility for our circumstances, both those we have inherited and those we have created. In doing so, we give in to fear and the survival-based conditioning that obscures our innate fundamental wisdom and compassion.

However, simply asking the magical Empowerment Zone question—What can I do?—throws open the door to the clear blue sky realm of the Empowerment Triangle, limitless possibility, and authentic relationship, regardless of the circumstances we face. This is how we become an unstoppable force for good in the world—by owning our choices and holding ourselves accountable. By choosing to no longer play the victim, we embrace the liberating power of the co-creative mind; by transforming our persecutors into challengers, we make necessary changes and learn how to challenge ourselves and others in empowering ways; and by letting go of the rescuer and our need to fix and save others, we encourage and support them side by side in the role of coach.

> This is how we become an unstoppable force for good in the world—by owning our choices and holding ourselves accountable.

WHEN OTHERS ARE IN REACTIVE-SURVIVAL MODE

You might think, "Well, it's all well and good for me to live and work in the Empowerment Zone, but what about all those Drama Zone people I have to deal with every day? Won't I just get mowed down, trying to live in a responsive-relational mode in a Drama Zone world?" That's a reasonable question, but one already loaded with some Drama Zone assumptions about others. Living in the Empowerment Zone has nothing to do with being naïve. It also has nothing to do with judging others as being in the Drama Zone. Rather, it has everything to do with compassionately recognizing when and where we fall into the Drama Zone and simply owning and shifting that. When we realize how easily we ourselves are pulled into habitual fear-based survival strategies and coping mechanisms, it allows us to experience compassion rather than judgment for other people who struggle with the challenges of the human condition, just as we do.

So, from an Empowerment Zone perspective, we focus on our side of the street and let others be responsible for theirs. When we own our own slips or dives into the Drama Zone, other people are often inspired to do the same. However, whether they clean up their side of the street or not is ultimately none of our business—we're only responsible for our side and remaining as accountable as possible. If we truly want to invite or inspire others into the Empowerment Zone, we can listen without judgment and express authentic interest in their experience and struggles. Doing so often encourages them to connect with their own basic goodness and wisdom. If we can create a blame-free environment of genuine caring, others are less likely to engage in fear-based, *reactive-survival mode* strategies to defend or protect themselves.

PREVENTING HARM AND SPEAKING TRUTH TO POWER

But what about more drastic circumstances? What do we do when others are actual threats or we witness them causing harm to others? That's where the final step of getting off the Drama Triangle comes in—make a boundary! Whenever actual physical, sexual, or emotional harm is occurring, prevention comes first. We need to make a boundary in the most effective and skillful way we can, but the immediate priority is always to stop the harm and prevent it from happening in the future, especially when the situation involves children or others who cannot defend themselves.

In our own lives, developing and maintaining clear boundaries tends to discourage harmful situations. People who chronically act in harmful ways generally avoid people with good boundaries. When making a necessary boundary, it's important to do so without becoming caught up in yet another Drama Triangle and the victim, persecutor, or rescuer mindsets. Nonetheless, preventing harm comes first; finding our way back to the Empowerment Zone comes second.

As discussed in chapter 10, when we actually experience victimization, seeking validation and support, choosing appropriate modes of healing, and sometimes pursuing a process of justice can empower us to move forward in our lives as survivors. Some helpful approaches to justice include the restorative and transformative models, as well as an overall spirit of harm reduction and prevention. The desire for revenge and punishment is often understandable, and it can truly feel like a legitimate expression of anger. However, I recommend reflecting on where the mind of vengeance will ultimately take us. Will taking action from that mindset actually meet our needs for healing and genuinely empower us to move forward as survivors?

In cases where someone in power is causing harm, it is absolutely within the Empowerment Zone context to call it out. In fact, we can more effectively speak truth to power when we embrace Empowerment Zone principles to bring about needed change, healing, and social transformation.

PART V

REALIZING THE
HEART-MIND AND
THE WAY FORWARD

13

DISCOVERING THE POWER OF COMPASSION AND RESILIENCE

Developing a kinder and more caring relationship with ourselves and others and increasing our capacity for courageous and compassionate engagement with life fortunately does not require us to give away everything, live in a monastery, and dedicate our lives to meditation and prayer (although that may be a wonderful life choice for some). As we explored earlier in the book, we humans are certainly hardwired for survival-based behaviors, but we're also hardwired for altruism.

We typically think of prosocial mind states such as empathy, caring, and compassion in terms of our relationships with others, but the truth is that it all begins at home. Developing a caring and compassionate relationship with ourselves is the ground for developing these prosocial qualities in our relationships with others. So in the following pages, please remember that we can simply place the prefix *self* in front of any of these prosocial attributes (as in *self-empathy* or *self-compassion*). Our capacity to recognize when we fall into reactive-survival mode in our relationships, and our ability to shift back to the Empowerment Zone and sphere of Authentic Relationship, depends on us developing radical compassion toward ourselves.

_____ **Neuroscience Note** _____

Researchers have identified neural circuitry associated with emotional empathy—our capacity to feel what others are feeling. As you might suspect, we're more likely to feel empathy for those we know and care about, and one of the stronger empathic relationships is that between parents and their children. Additionally, the reward circuitry in our brains is activated not only by helping others but also by witnessing other people's altruistic behaviors. In other words, we are wired for empathy and rewarded for helping behaviors.[1]

CULTIVATING THE PROSOCIAL QUALITIES OF THE HEART-MIND

Most of us likely know people who seem naturally kind and giving—perhaps someone in our community who is always doing good deeds: bringing homeless people hot food, visiting the elderly, or reaching out to neighbors who are ill. We see these individuals perform these acts of kindness quietly, without fanfare, as if it were the most natural thing to do. They don't appear to be doing it for recognition or out of some kind of religious sentiment. Apparently they just do it because they are wired that way. We might think that such people are the exception—even saints, in some cases. But the fact is that we are all wired for instinctual empathy, compassion, and altruistic behaviors; it's just that other factors sometimes get in our way.

> Our survival on this planet depends on our ability to be more compassionate toward each other.

Culturally, most of us grew up with the widely held belief that humans are naturally selfish, competitive, and greedy. It's not hard to see how such a collective negative view of human nature becomes a self-fulfilling prophecy. If we expect others to operate from a default mode of self-centeredness, we might then conclude that it would be naïve not to focus primarily on getting our own needs met, even at the expense of others, since that appears to be how the game is played. Though we still hear about positive values of respect, kindness, and compassion in the public square, our modern winner-take-all culture is actually centered around the worship of wealth, celebrity, power, and—above all—winning at all costs. We propagate this negative outlook on human nature to our significant detriment and peril. For this reason, the current brain science regarding our capacities for altruistic behaviors is critical.

The Dalai Lama—a world-renowned voice for peace, nonviolence, and compassion—explains:

> From my own limited experience, I have found that
> the greatest degree of inner tranquility comes from the
> development of love and compassion. . . . Ultimately,
> the reason why love and compassion bring the greatest
> happiness is simply that our nature cherishes them above
> all else. The need for love lies at the very foundation
> of human existence. It results from the profound
> interdependence we all share with one another.[2]

His Holiness has been an active partner with scientists, contemplatives, and yogis from around the world for decades. Relying on the wisdom of thousands of years of contemplative traditions, as well as more recent technology such as advanced brain imaging and the immunoassay technique, this ongoing dialogue (hosted by the Mind & Life Institute) strives to better understand the neurobiology underlying human emotions and actions in order to promote our innate proclivities for kindness, compassion, and altruistic behavior.

Let's face it—our survival on this planet depends on our ability to be more compassionate toward each other. If we can't do this, we will eventually be unable to equitably share Earth's limited resources of quality air, water, food, and energy. As leaders around the world have been warning us, compassion is no longer a luxury. Actually, it never was. This is the reason why compassion has become a hot topic in affective neuroscience research. There is growing recognition that our world is reaching a tipping point, where increasing our individual and collective access to prosocial mind states is not only the key to reversing the damage we have created through unchecked greed, exploitation, and consumerism, but it's also essential to our survival. Now that we face the reality of a potential endgame—given the dangers of an environmental catastrophe caused by climate change and nuclear war—we can no longer afford to put our own needs and wants ahead of others'. We are clearly all in this together. Our complete and complex interdependence with each other and the environment becomes more obvious with each passing day.

Some of us may feel the need to cultivate these prosocial mind states for more immediate personal reasons: a general dissatisfaction with our lives; the pain of internalized trauma, shame, and oppression; increasing isolation; and loss of community. Perhaps we just feel the need to care because deep down inside we always have.

Whatever your aspirations—to be happier, enjoy more rewarding relationships, create more abundance or financial security, or help establish a more equitable and sustainable global society—you can begin by recognizing the futility and destructive nature of fear-based, *reactive-survival mode* (Drama Zone) coping strategies. And from there you can begin to cultivate your potential for caring, compassionate, and altruistic behaviors in service of co-creating a more enlightened society for all—a healthy and sustainable world that we can pass on to our children and grandchildren.

Thankfully, we already possess powerful tools for fostering prosocial mind states. These tools have stood the test of time for thousands of years, as well as the rigors of modern scientific investigation. Cultivating greater empathy and compassion for our own and others' very human struggles is a great place to begin. In this chapter we will learn proven methods for doing just that.

EMPATHY

We took a look at the difference between empathy and compassion in chapter 3 when looking at Daniel Goleman's social awareness quadrant. The distinction is worth revisiting here in the context of cultivating the heart-mind. The word *empathy* is relatively new in the English language. In 1908, two psychologists—one from Cornell University and the other from Cambridge University—coined it as a translation of the German term *einfühlung*, combining the Greek *em*, meaning "in," with *pathos*, meaning "feeling." The meaning and use of *empathy* have varied over time, but for the purpose of Radical Responsibility, I like to define it as the capacity to feel with relative accuracy what another is feeling, not simply through making an observational assessment, but by actually experiencing similar feelings in oneself.

In other words, when we feel the happiness or distress of another person, we may actually experience happiness or distress ourselves. What we do with that experience is another matter all together. Sensing another's happiness could, on the one hand, produce feelings of *sympathetic joy*, a traditional Buddhist term that means we are happy for another person's happiness. On the other hand, it could lead to feelings of envy, jealously, resentment, or unworthiness. Sensing another's distress could possibly lead to feelings of sympathy, concern, or compassion, but it could also lead to empathic distress, overload, and burnout.

Our capacity to feel what others are feeling is sometimes referred to as *resonating* with others. *Resonance* as a scientific term describes how vibrating systems impact one another in terms of the amplitude and frequency of oscillations and how one system can become entrained with another. Resonance occurs with all types of waves or vibrations—mechanical, acoustical, optical, electromagnetic, fluid, and so forth.

Psychotherapists use the term *empathic resonance* to describe a therapist's ability to provide a client with the experience of being seen and understood. The therapist employs observational skills, clinical experience, and empathy to intuit what the client is experiencing and needing, and conveys that back to the client so that the client feels heard and witnessed. In psychiatrist Daniel J. Siegel's words, the client *feels felt*, an experience that has tremendous potential for fostering healing and improved integration of brain function.[3]

COMPASSION

As I briefly touched on in chapter 3 and above, empathy doesn't necessarily lead to compassion—that is, the desire to alleviate the suffering of others. The English word *compassion* can be traced back to the Latin prefix *com* or *cum*, meaning "with," and the Latin verb *pati*, meaning "to suffer." Thus *compassion* literally means "to suffer with." In order to better understand the roots of compassionate behavior and how to cultivate greater compassion, I believe it helps to define compassion more precisely as a caring response to another's distress or suffering. This can take two forms:

1. being willing "to suffer with" another; to bear witness and not turn away in the face of their distress; to accompany and provide solace to them through one's caring presence.

2. acting to alleviate or mitigate another person's distress or suffering.

The first form of compassion described above is critical to any genuinely compassionate response to another's suffering. In some instances, this may be all we can do in the moment, or it may be the most truly supportive thing to do for someone in pain. Any rush to fix or alleviate another's suffering—unless it is something as simple as lending a hand to someone who has fallen or calling for help in a medical emergency—may, in fact, be more about alleviating our own empathic distress. However, the willingness to patiently accompany another in their time of suffering with care and awareness—while realizing it is not one's own, and despite feeling empathic distress—may be the necessary means for discovering how we can best help that person.

Neuroscience Note

Daniel J. Siegel and other researchers have found that caring presence can promote healing for the recipient as well as for the person embodying caring presence, because it promotes greater holistic integration among the brain's diverse and disparate neural networks. In other words, proactively offering our empathic and caring presence to someone who is suffering, though it might take the form of simply sitting silently at their bedside, is an act of active compassion.[4]

So compassion is the willingness to be with suffering—our own and that of others—without resentment, blame, or other fear-based, *reactive-survival mode* behaviors that will just make the situation worse. *Acceptance* is key to embracing suffering, our own and others', in responsive-relational mode as well as a radical act of self-empowerment. We can actually recognize that suffering is part of life and not translate its presence in ways that create even more drama. I'm not talking about indulging or justifying suffering but rather working with it from an Empowerment Zone perspective. I think of the Serenity Prayer here, which could just as easily be called the Wisdom Prayer: "God, grant me the serenity to accept the things I cannot change, the courage to change the things I can, and the wisdom to know the difference."

The power of acceptance can't be overestimated. Accepting the basic fact of the suffering and pain we witness, as well as our own empathic distress in response, and remaining willing to experience it is what allows us to access our innate capacities for compassion. Our initial impulse may be to turn away from suffering. Our empathic sensitivity may even trigger avoidance mechanisms or fight-flight-freeze responses. We may find ourselves withdrawing in fear or lashing out in anger. However, we can also recognize our empathic distress as the initial response of our empathy-caring-compassion circuitry; it's simply the natural response of our tender and vulnerable heart to the pain of others. Doing so will help us shift away from a threat-avoidance response, move into a healthy stress response, and discover the courage to move from empathy to compassion.

As we learn to recognize our experiences of empathetic distress as the first sign of our compassion response, we develop even more confidence in our basic goodness, which, in turn, provides access to increased interpersonal resonance, leading to enhanced neural integration in our brain and nervous system, as well as a boost in overall well-being and resilience. That's quite a payoff! And it all starts with holding our seat and feeling whatever arises when the going gets tough.

Living bravely with empathic awareness means that when I encounter someone's sadness, it touches me—I care and resonate with their feelings. It's more than a disinterested observation of what another person is experiencing; it actually opens my heart. This doesn't mean that I have to respond in some way, or even that a response would be helpful. It does mean that I'm living courageously with an open heart and developing greater confidence in my own and others' basic humanity.

> Our own healing and transformation depend on accepting ourselves as we are in the moment.

My sincere hope is that this chapter will show how we can choose to generate a positive relational approach to ourselves, to our lives, and to others. We don't have to be victims of our conditioning or even our genetics. We also don't need to remain victims of mishap, illness, or handicap. There are countless examples of people facing the worst circumstances imaginable who have chosen to rise above their situation with self-compassion and bravery. We can do that too. It's all right there within our reach. And we can start by making use of the tools and practices that follow.

FOUR IMMEASURABLES: LOVING-KINDNESS, COMPASSION, SYMPATHETIC JOY, AND EQUANIMITY

The four *bramaviharas*, often translated as the four "immeasurables," refers to four boundless or immeasurable qualities of the awakened heart-mind and an ancient set of Buddhist practices meant to promote the qualities and prosocial capacities we've been exploring. People have been using these practices for several thousand years, and current research in neuroscience has confirmed their value in today's world. We are going to explore each of them in turn, as simple yet powerful practices for transforming our own neurobiology and developing our innate qualities of wisdom and compassion.

Loving-Kindness

For all of us, love can be the natural state of our own being; naturally at peace, naturally connected, because this becomes the reflection of who we simply are. **SHARON SALZBERG**

As I mentioned in the last chapter, loving-kindness (also known as unconditional friendliness) comes from the Pali word *metta* and the Sanskrit term *maitri*. The American Buddhist teacher Sharon Salzberg has been a leading proponent and beloved teacher of this contemplative practice, which has gained numerous adherents in the West. Traditionally, loving-kindness refers to a warm, friendly, and non-judgmental relationship with ourselves and others. For ourselves, loving-kindness begins with deeply accepting ourselves, recognizing our basic humanity, and acknowledging the unconditional basic goodness underlying even our most difficult challenges. Our own healing and transformation depend on accepting ourselves as we are in the moment—the good, the bad, and the ugly. And as discussed in this book, that acceptance goes hand in hand with letting go of patterns that no longer serve us.

The formal loving-kindness practice involves reciting (aloud or silently) a series of statements: May I be safe. May I be happy (or peaceful). May I be healthy. May I be at ease. We usually begin with ourselves as the beneficiaries of these statements, but since offering loving-kindness to ourselves can prove challenging for some of us, it may be easier to begin with someone with whom it's easy to open our heart—our child, partner, or someone close who's in a lot of pain; a benefactor such as a parent, teacher, or anyone for whom we feel a lot of gratitude. As a young boy, one of my teachers saw a puppy being stoned to death; it was an experience that broke his heart completely. As he grew up, this experience became an empowering starting point for his loving-kindness practice.

If you choose to begin this practice by focusing on others, simply substitute *you* for *I* in the statements above—for example, May you be peaceful. You can also address the particular person by name: Rosa, may you be peaceful. Mom, may you be healthy. You'll find different versions of these statements and variations of the practice online. (I recommend using Sharon Salzberg, the Dalai Lama, Thich Nhat Hanh, and Pema Chödrön as resources.)

Extending loving-kindness to oneself or to close loved ones is only the beginning of the practice. Traditionally we work with five types of recipients:

- ourselves

- a benefactor

- a neutral person

- a difficult person

- an enemy

After working with ourselves or a benefactor, we can work with someone toward whom we feel neutral, then with someone with whom we have some personal difficulty, and finally with someone for whom we have truly difficult feelings (fear, hate, and so on). That last step can prove difficult, so it's helpful to work our way up to it. I'll also note here that we'll be following the same progression in the practices intended to promote compassion, sympathetic joy, and equanimity.

So that's how it's traditionally done, but you can create a version that works for you. You certainly don't need to work with all these groups in a particular session, and you can choose whatever seems to work best in the moment, for whomever you feel called to include in your practice. I recommend doing the loving-kindness practice in the middle of a mindfulness meditation session, as it will help you open your heart at the beginning and assist you in letting go at the end. That being said, please feel free to do this practice anytime, anywhere—intentionally while taking a walk, for example, or spontaneously whenever you feel inspired.

There's also a concluding part of the practice in which you extend loving-kindness to all creatures everywhere, including yourself, by repeating the following statements: May I and all beings be safe. May I and all beings be happy. May I and all beings be healthy. May I and all beings be at ease.

Okay, so that's how the practice goes. Let's give it a try.

EXERCISE   Loving-Kindness Practice

Find a sitting posture that feels naturally uplifted and dignified and also relaxed and stable. To begin, work with basic mindfulness of body and breath until you feel relatively settled. Cultivate the qualities of interoceptive awareness (awareness of internal sensations) we have worked on in earlier exercises in order to establish a quality of embodied presence. When you are ready, begin with the loving-kindness statements presented below, beginning with yourself, a benefactor, or someone for whom your heart easily opens. Recite the statements to yourself silently while maintaining a light attentiveness to your body and the sensations of breathing:

- May I (you) be safe.

- May I (you) be happy (or peaceful).

- May I (you) be healthy.

- May I (you) be at ease.

If beginning with yourself, see if you can let the statements drop into your body, actually feeling safe, peaceful, happy, healthy, and at ease. Even if it feels overly conceptual at first, just stay with the practice, reciting the statements silently at your own pace and simply feeling whatever arises. And if you choose to start with one of the people described above, visualize them in your mind's eye in front of you and imagine that the positive energy of the statements radiates out from your heart center to that person as you recite the statements. Finish the practice for yourself or the other person (that is, the benefactor or someone with whom it's easy to open your heart) and then switch. When you've done both, wrap it up with the concluding step—wish all these qualities for all beings, including yourself.

As you learn and progress with this practice, you could experiment working with a neutral person or someone with whom you have difficulty. Just go at your own pace and let your ability to extend loving-kindness grow with time. Always conclude the practice with the final series, though: May I and all beings be safe. May I and all beings be happy. And so on.

If becoming kinder to oneself and others were not motivation enough, current research points to a host of tangible ways in which doing these practices improves our overall physical, mental, and emotional health, as well as our quality of life. Citing multiple scientific studies, Emma Seppälä—a Stanford-based researcher, psychologist, and author of *The Happiness Track: How to Apply the Science of Happiness to Accelerate Your Success*—lists the following benefits of loving-kindness practice:

- more positive emotions and fewer negative emotions

- increased vagal tone (known to boost mood and feelings of social connection)

- fewer migraines and reduced chronic pain

- diminished symptoms of PTSD

- increased emotional intelligence

- more gray matter in areas of the brain associated with emotion regulation

- enhanced empathy and compassion

- improved social connectedness

- reduced implicit bias toward minorities

- fewer depressive symptoms[5]

More good news: The research indicates that loving-kindness practice has measurable effects even in small doses (say, after a ten-minute session). Additionally, participants in loving-kindness studies showed positive effects in a follow-up measure fifteen months later.[6] In other words, loving-kindness practice works—short-term and long-term.

Compassion

We've discussed compassion (*karuna* in Pali) quite a bit already, so let's jump right in to the practices. As I mentioned in the loving-kindness instructions, it's helpful to sandwich the practice of contemplating these phrases in the middle of a session of mindfulness meditation (say, five to twenty minutes before and five to ten afterward). Doing so will help you settle your mind and foster a stable, openhearted presence. However, feel free to try these practices anytime, anywhere.

Feel free to adapt these statements in ways that work for you. You can do the practice as a self-compassion meditation, a meditation for others, or both. You can also divide up your time between the different statements however you like; you can even just focus on a few of them. The important thing is to make the practice meaningful for you. Regardless of whether you experience increased feelings of compassion or not, just continue and trust that the practice will provide benefits. And if you experience some resistance in doing the practice, that's fine—it's all part of it. Just keep going.

The more we soak our minds in compassionate thoughts, the more we begin to rewire our brains to a default mode of not only greater empathy and compassion, but overall well-being and happiness.

EXERCISE   Compassion Contemplations for Working with Enmity

The following practice is for those of us who struggle with hard feelings toward another person—someone we know personally, a stranger, or even a public figure of some sort. If you feel interested in this practice, couch it between short mindfulness sessions, bring the person clearly to mind, and recite the following statements to yourself:

- Just like me, this person was once an innocent child.

- Just like me, this person has basic goodness.

- Just like me, this person wants to be happy.

- Just like me, this person has been hurt and disappointed many times.

- Just like me, this person suffers.

- Just like me, this person needs love.

- May this person be free of suffering.

- May this person awaken to the fundamental goodness within them.

- May this person no longer cause suffering.

- May this person be happy and at ease.

- May we all be free of suffering.

- May we all be happy and at ease.

Recite and contemplate these statements for as long as you are comfortable doing so, or perhaps a bit longer. Notice if any shifts occur in your feelings toward this person, but also stay patient—shifts often occur whether we're conscious of them or not. As with all these exercises, trust that people just like you have been reaping the profound benefits of these practices for several thousand years, benefits that are now being confirmed by rigorous science. There are a number of compassion meditation practices being studied at major universities and research institutes, and the compelling results are quite similar to those listed above for the loving-kindness practice.[7]

Sympathetic Joy

The more we care for the happiness of others, the greater our own sense of well-being becomes. Cultivating a close, warm-hearted feeling for others automatically puts the mind at ease. This helps remove whatever fears or insecurities we may have and gives us the strength to cope with any obstacles we encounter. It is the ultimate source of success in life. **HIS HOLINESS THE 14TH DALAI LAMA**

Sympathetic joy (*mudita* in Pali) refers to the joy we feel for another person's good fortune, success, or happiness. Based on the realization that we are all interconnected, we see the happiness and joy of others as inseparable from our own. Of course, sometimes we can get a little jealous or resentful when good things come to other people—that's to be expected, given our fear- and survival-based conditioning. We might consider, however, that rewiring our brains to increase our capacity for sympathetic joy with the following practice might just be in our own enlightened self-interest (that is, our healthy, long-term interest).

Think about it—if you feel happy when good things happen to you *and* you feel happy when good things happen to others, that's a whole lot of happiness going around!

EXERCISE   Sympathetic Joy Practice

As before, it's helpful to first establish an embodied and open-hearted presence through basic mindfulness of body and breathing. To begin the sympathetic joy contemplative practice, reflect on or visualize a happy or successful friend and review the blessings and good fortune they have experienced. Then silently repeat and contemplate the following phrases while maintaining a light attention on your body and the sensations of breathing:

- I'm joyful that you're happy.

- May your happiness continue.

- May your happiness increase.

- May your good fortune continue to shine.

- May your happiness and good fortune not leave you.

- May your good fortune continue undiminished.

- May your happiness continue undiminished.

Pause after each phrase and allow the words to reverberate in your heart. Whatever you experience—even resistance—is fine. Remember, it's just part of the practice.

Just as with the loving-kindness meditation, try working with various categories of people in your sympathetic joy practice: start from the easiest, move through to the most difficult, and wrap up the session by including all beings. If you have time, remember to conclude your practice session with some mindfulness meditation to let it soak in and help dissolve any excessive or difficult thoughts that have come up. Doing this practice regularly will help rewire your brain for more positivity, well-being, and happiness.

Equanimity

These well-known lines from a classic Zen teaching called *Hsin Hsin Ming*, or "Verses on the Faith-Mind," describe the profound meaning of *equanimity*, the fourth and final immeasurable. *Upekkha* in Pali, equanimity is what provides the ground for the other qualities of loving-kindness, compassion, and sympathetic joy to arise naturally in the mind. *Equanimity* means "balance" and "impartiality"; we relax our preferential mind and cool the fires of reactivity. With the mind's innate quality of—and capacity for—equanimity, we can allow things to simply be as they are, receiving everything equally without preference for one thing or another. Equanimity is not the same as indifference; it's a steady, invested mind that sees clearly. The radiant calm of the equanimous heart-mind naturally allows loving-kindness, compassion, and sympathetic joy to shine forth freely.

Equanimity also helps us avoid the rescuer position on the Drama Triangle by respecting the autonomy of others while at the same time wishing them happiness. With genuine equanimity, we can cultivate the other three immeasurables in an Empowerment Zone context.

EXERCISE   Equanimity Contemplative Practice

As always, begin and end your practice with some mindfulness meditation. Let your attention stabilize and contact an embodied, openhearted presence. Recite these phrases silently to yourself and extend them to the various groups of people described before—that is, a loved one or benefactor, a neutral person, a difficult person or an enemy, followed by all beings:

- Regardless of my wishes for you, your happiness is not in my hands.

- All beings are responsible for their own actions and happiness.

- Your happiness and unhappiness depend on your actions, not on my wishes.

- You are the inheritor of your own actions.

- May you do what needs to be done to find happiness.

As you work with these phrases, pay close attention to your state of mind and heart for the different people or beings on which you're focusing. The phrases will keep you grounded in equanimity, as opposed to indifference. You can also do this practice with yourself as the subject, remembering that circumstances are neutral and fostering your own equanimity and Radical Responsibility. After wrapping up your practice with some mindfulness meditation, appreciate any sensations of calm, clarity, and balance that have arisen for you.

FROM ME TO *MWE* (ME + WE)

In short, the mind is an embodied and relational process that regulates the flow of energy and information. **DANIEL J. SIEGEL**

Daniel J. Siegel, who contributed the foreword to this book, is a leading voice in our current understanding of the mind, affective and contemplative neuroscience, and an emerging field known as interpersonal neurobiology, which synthesizes research from anthropology, biology, computer science, mathematics, neuroscience, psychology, and systems theory (among other fields). He is also the author of numerous groundbreaking books: *The Whole-Brain Child*, *Brainstorm*, *Mindsight*, *The Developing Mind*, and *Aware: The Science and Practice of Presence*, to name a few. Siegel's work has been a major influence on my own, and I'd like to end this chapter by looking closer at his work on our understanding of the mind, the brain, the self, and the interpersonal or relational domains in which we live and function.

People change us; we change each other.

Siegel describes optimal brain function in terms of both differentiation and integration. To meet the challenges of modern life, we develop increasingly differentiated and complex neural networks across distinct regions of the brain. Ideally, we also experience increasing levels of integration among these parts and networks in order for the whole brain system to communicate and operate most efficiently.[8]

Neuroscience Note

Neuroscientists have employed functional MRI and PET scans to examine the brains of advanced meditators who have logged more than ten thousand hours of practice. What they find, especially when they ask an adept to enter a meditative state, is that their entire brain lights up with an integrated symphonic display. These meditators are also known to experience paranormal abilities such as clairvoyance. Apparently the more differentiated, synchronized, and attuned our brain is, the less it's confined to the boundaries of our body.[9]

Influenced by culture and mainstream science, we tend to view the self as an isolated entity that is separate from others. Siegel asserts that this belief in a skin-encapsulated *self* represents a form of impaired integration.[10] As his definition above indicates, Siegel views the human mind as a process of energy and information transfer that is both embodied and part of an interconnected web of relationships. This notion is not a stretch on either a logical or intuitive level. Who would we be if we were independent of our relationships, especially our close ones?

My beloved spiritual teacher and mentor died in 1987, two years into my fourteen-year prison sentence. I lost both of my parents to cancer, one just before I was released from prison and the other shortly after. Since leaving prison, I lost two life partners—both amazing women—to cancer. With each of these difficult losses I experienced significant disorientation and loss of self. It took considerable time, especially after my beloved partner Denise died in 2008, for a relatively stable sense of self to emerge embedded within the framework of my ongoing relationships. Today, I am incredibly fortunate to have my partner Sophie in my life. We have been together for about four years, and I can still feel my sense of self reshaping itself within a new relational field that includes this incredible woman, as well as her wonderful French-Canadian family in Quebec. Most of us have experienced shifts like this. People change us; we change each other. It's hard to imagine a self that isn't influenced by other people, places, and events.

Siegel asserts that we are both a differentiated *Me* with a particular personal history as well as an embodied experience and an interconnected *We*—a process and flow of relationships. Throughout time, spiritual teachers, philosophers, and other visionaries have encouraged us to shift our locus of self-orientation from *Me* to *We* in service of a more global consciousness that recognizes our profound interdependence with each other, our planet, and all of life. This is a laudable aspiration. However, Siegel suggests that we need not—and ought not—leave *Me* behind to embrace the *We*. No matter how *We*-focused we may become, we're still responsible for taking care of the embodied *Me*. Thus Seigel suggests combining the two into *MWe*. To break that down into an equation: *Me* + *We* = *MWe*.[11]

Embracing *MWe* consciousness, we see our embodied self as simply one node in a vast relational heart-mind-life network—an Indra's net in which every facet contains the whole, resonating with all the other nodes and the entire net itself with symphonic harmony. To participate in this expanded sense of a relationship-centered self, we need to consciously and responsibly occupy and embody the mechanical and conditioned bottom-up body-brain as well as the more conscious top-down body-brain. More importantly, we need to engage the fully conscious and intersubjective heart-mind that is capable of connecting with others in a sphere of mutuality and co-created social cohesion. To survive our imperiled world—much less thrive in it—this is a matter of great urgency.

By embracing Radical Responsibility, we own our accountability both to the embodied self (or *Me*) and to our network of interconnections with others, life, and the planet itself (*We*). As Siegel says, from the perspective of *MWe*, caring for others and the planet *is* caring for the self. The pieces are inseparable from the whole. By taking care of *Me*, Radical Responsibility provides access to the genuine vulnerability and bravery of the heart-mind of *MWe*—the Empowerment Zone domain of Authentic Relationship. In doing so, we open the pearly gates to "the better angels of our nature"[12]—empathic resonance, love, courage, genuine altruism, and compassion.

Until one is committed, there is hesitancy, the chance to draw back, always ineffectiveness. Concerning all acts of initiative (and creation) there is one elementary truth, the ignorance of which kills countless ideas and splendid plans: that the moment one definitely commits oneself, then Providence moves too. All sorts of things occur to help one that would never otherwise have occurred. **W. H. MURRAY**

14

DESIGNING AND SUSTAINING A TRANSFORMATIONAL LIFE

Welcome to the final chapter in our journey together. Having made it this far, you are likely inspired by some of the ideas and practices we've explored here. You probably also realize that this journey we have taken together is only the beginning, and that true progress will require commitment, practice, and patience. Whether you follow the steps as outlined in this book chapter by chapter or simply choose to focus on the exercises that are most meaningful for you, I strongly encourage you to develop a clear game plan. In this chapter we will explore tried-and-true principles and methods for transformational change, providing all the inspiration and structure you need to develop a powerful life plan for yourself. You will find even more resources at the end of this chapter (see Additional Resources for Your Path).

Are you ready to design the most fabulous life you could imagine? Countless human beings just like you and me have refused to listen to the naysayers, both internal and external, and found the courage to create the life of their dreams. So why not you? Please grab your Radical Responsibility journal and start a new section titled "My Game Plan," and then begin working your way through the following steps.

1. DEFINING YOUR LIFE PURPOSE

Remember the saying from chapter 2, "You either learn to ride the donkey or the donkey rides you"? In much the same way, we either design our lives or our lives design us. A key step in designing our life is getting clear about our life's purpose, and this requires answering some crucial questions:

- Who am I?

- Why was I born?

- What is life all about?

- What's important to me?

- What is life asking of me?

Exploring these questions has led me to articulate my own life purpose in this way:

> **Long version** To awaken from the trance of fear-based, conditioned existence and live as consciously, fearlessly, and compassionately as I can in order to alleviate suffering and contribute lasting value at the greatest scale of which I'm capable.

> **Short version** To awaken, to love, and to serve.

These statements—and the personal conviction that fuels them—guide the countless decisions I make, small and large, day in and day out. They also inform how I prioritize daily life and work activities, providing me with a clear internal compass and a deep feeling of alignment and integrity. This clarity of life purpose got me safely through fourteen years in a maximum security prison and set the stage for an exciting and fulfilling postprison career. Anytime I find myself veering off course, internal alarms go off, reminding me to refocus on my deepest aspirations.

EXERCISE   Life Purpose

Please set this book down and title the next blank page in your Radical Responsibility journal "My Life Purpose." You could start by answering the questions in the list above. You may need to revisit this writing again and again over the next few weeks as you explore and clarify your life purpose. Please take your time with this exercise—it's incredibly important. Whatever you come up with, put it in your own words and make it yours. Reading your life purpose statement to yourself should fill you with inspiration. If it doesn't, you're not there yet. Just keep working on it until the phrasing excites you.

2. BECOMING A PRACTITIONER

We know that it's all too easy to let the challenges and vicissitudes of daily life carry us along willy-nilly with no clear path. If we don't make the commitment to get in the driver's seat and take ownership for our life's direction on a daily basis, something or someone else will. Being a *practitioner* and having a *path* means acknowledging that the life we envision for ourselves is not going to happen by accident or wishful thinking. On the contrary, it requires commitment and a consistent daily practice.

Burn the boats!

The term *practitioner* invokes a powerful archetype signifying your commitment to excellence and mastery. By fully embracing the practitioner archetype, you can establish a new identity for yourself—one that includes a powerful set of values and priorities. Truly becoming a practitioner requires clear purpose, relentless commitment, oceans of patience, and, of course, practice! It also involves embracing what I call the *spirit of mastery*.

With clarity about your life purpose, you can design the life you want and begin organizing your time and priorities accordingly. It's like having a bright star to guide your journey, helping you navigate even the most treacherous waters. It allows you to address and integrate all the various dimensions of your life—health, relationships, livelihood, spiritual life, and everything else—into a cohesive way of showing up in the world.

Staying true to your life's purpose requires commitment. There is a certain way in which the universe seems to test you when you create an intention around change or accomplishing something—the bigger your vision, the bigger the obstacles. When we stay the course and remain true to our intention, the universe then often appears to support us. The stars line up in all kinds of serendipitous ways as described in the earlier quote by the mountaineer and writer W. H. Murray in *The Scottish Himalayan Expedition*. That cycle often repeats itself in various ways; the universe has a way of continually testing your commitment and resolve.

However, until we really commit, until we burn the boats, so to speak, not much happens. As the story goes, after coming ashore in a new land, Alexander the Great had his troops burn all their boats to motivate them to victory; without a means of escape, they had no choice but to succeed in battle or die trying. Are you willing to fully commit and burn the boats in order to achieve your life's purpose? What would burning the boats mean for you?

EXERCISE   Burn the Boats

Grab your Radical Responsibility journal and start a new section titled "Burn the Boats." Then write down anything that comes to mind when you consider this level of commitment. Keep working on this until you feel a crystal-clear sense of what burning the boats means to you. Any time you feel that commitment wavering, revisit this exercise.

Manifesting our life's purpose is a marathon, not a sprint. The journey requires tremendous patience. There will be exciting breakthroughs and seemingly fast-paced change. However, more often than not, change and progress will be slow and steady, and sometimes you may feel as if you have hit a plateau where not much is happening. You may even feel as if you have hit a wall. This is when we need patience and resolve to just keep going, trusting the journey and believing in our purpose.

Let's talk about practice itself. You know beyond a shadow of a doubt that developing any new skill requires practice. Think about learning how to play a new musical instrument—none of us would imagine that we could become proficient, much less masterful, without lots of practice. Strangely though, we often assume or secretly wish that personal or spiritual growth would happen of its own accord or by accident somehow. It's almost as if we have a sense of entitlement when it comes to these domains in our lives. So let's disabuse ourselves of any such notion right here, right now. In any human endeavor, progress and success require diligent and effective practice.

Practice has two principal dimensions: doing it and doing it effectively. Let's investigate this using the mindfulness practices we explored in the preceding chapters. Since mindfulness practice is foundational to the path of Radical Responsibility, this is a good place to begin.

Expect the resistance and use it as your friend.

To develop a consistent daily mindfulness meditation practice, you first need a place to do it. It's extremely helpful to have a dedicated space in your home for meditation practice. I have a room just steps away from my bedroom where my partner, Sophie, and I practice together every morning before breakfast. Of course, depending on your living situation, it may not be possible to dedicate an entire room to meditation practice. Nonetheless, you may be able to dedicate part of a room. I know several people who have a dedicated space for practice in their bedroom. The more visible the reminders of your practice commitment, the better.

During my early prison years when I was living in big dormitories, I chose to stay on the top bunk even though the lower bunk was preferred and viewed as a perk of seniority. The lower bunk lacked headroom for sitting, but I could sit on the top bunk relatively undisturbed late at night. Eventually I started sitting in the trash closet at the entrance to the dorm. I would clean it up and place the trash cans, brooms, and mops temporarily outside and then sit on a metal folding chair in the closet, which had a small window in the door. People would see me and wonder what the heck I was doing, but they left me alone for the most part. This closet was like a sauna in the heat of summer, but I was committed, to say the least—driven, actually.

You also need a time to practice. Most people find it ideal to practice first thing in the morning before the onslaught of daily activities and life's distractions. This is certainly true for me. I have a very demanding schedule that kicks in at 9 a.m. every morning and often extends into the evening hours. Sometimes, when pressed for time in the morning, I tell myself, "I don't have time now—I'll just practice later in the day." That later-in-the-day rarely happens. So I've learned to stick to my morning practice schedule. You need to figure out for yourself the ideal time to do your practice. The length of time you practice isn't as important—even ten minutes of mindfulness will get your day off to a great start.

You also need a strategy to outwit the resistance that will inevitably arise. Lots of people say something like "Whenever I manage to sit down to practice, I enjoy it and feel much better afterward, but it's still hard to get myself to do it—something always gets in the way." This is a common experience. My advice here is to expect the resistance and use it as your friend. If you commit to practicing meditation at a certain time each day, more often than not you will start experiencing thoughts of resistance as that time approaches: "I don't really need to." "I'm not feeling well today." "It's okay if I skip it today." "It's actually good to take a day off here and there." "I don't want to be too rigid about it." And so on.

When these thoughts come up, I've trained myself to recognize them as helpful reminders: "Oh, there's the resistance thoughts—must be time to practice." However you work with this phenomenon, the important thing is to expect the resistance and inoculate yourself to it in some way. When these thoughts arise, they're just thoughts. There's no need to take them seriously or believe them.

So that covers the first dimension of practice—actually doing it. The second aspect, practicing effectively, refers to technique. Practicing with proper and efficient technique is critical to progress and success in anything. If we practice hitting golf balls or shooting baskets again and again with poor technique, we're simply developing bad habits. Whatever we do with enough repetition will become grooved in our neurobiology as a habit, so practicing with good technique is essential.

I've described the mindfulness meditation techniques in earlier chapters, so I won't go into depth here except to emphasize three things:

1. Begin each practice session with a clear benevolent intention—something such as "I intend to develop wakefulness in order to enjoy and add value to life."

2. Work on developing good posture. It can take a while to find and develop a relatively erect posture that feels naturally uplifted and dignified and, at the same time, relaxed and stable.

3. Do your best to let go of ambition, striving, and any form of self-criticism. Instead, cultivate qualities such as curiosity, self-acceptance, and humor.

Whatever form of mindfulness you choose to practice, it's extremely important to get expert instruction and to regularly check your technique with teachers or other guides.

For me, another critical element to truly embodying the practitioner archetype is developing the *spirit of mastery*, which means never settling for "good enough." It also means embracing the mindset of a lifelong learner. We realize at some point that we are here to learn, and that learning gives our life meaning. Just to be clear, the spirit of mastery has nothing to do with ambition, perfectionism, or recognition. Instead, it values the journey itself and recognizes that practice is the goal. We can work at perfecting an art or skill while at the same time realizing that the greatest value lies in the effort itself rather than reaching the goal. The spirit of mastery involves a love of learning and the ability to appreciate each moment of practice as the actualization of our human destiny—to train, grow, thrive, and awaken.

EXERCISE   Practice Record

Please create a practice record tool for yourself in calendar format. You may want to acquire a pocket-sized calendar with enough space in each day to record the practices you've done and the time dedicated to them. The important thing is to document daily your practices and the time spent on them, and to keep this practice record front and center on your radar so that you can't avoid it or kid yourself about how consistently you're practicing. Create a system that works for you and stick to it.

---

3. DISCOVERING OR DEVELOPING YOUR PATH

Having a clear sense of your path is the best safeguard against being sidetracked by old habits or life's constant distractions. Consistent progress requires not only clarity of purpose, strong commitment, patience, and practice, but also a good map to guide us. All the great spiritual traditions offer excellent maps for the journey. If you decide to embrace one of these, you will still need to refine and personalize the map for your own life circumstances. Whether you decide to follow a traditional spiritual path or construct your own, the principles and practices of Radical Responsibility we have explored together will accelerate your progress considerably.

In some ways, the spiritual journey, regardless of the particular path one chooses, is basically a journey of developing greater and greater confidence—particularly confidence in our own basic goodness and the innate goodness of others, society, and life itself. When we have that confidence, we naturally generate the four C's of prosocial behavior—caring, compassion, cooperation, and collaboration—as well as kindness, altruism, and stewardship. All of these contribute to a healthier and more sustainable world. On the flip side, when we don't have this confidence, we're susceptible to being overtaken by fear and enacting survival-based dynamics that increase suffering and imperil ourselves and others, including the planet. The world's great contemplative traditions all point to the sacredness of life and the divinity or inherent goodness of our essential nature. As we saw in chapter 1, discovering our basic goodness is the ultimate source of strength and resilience for our human journey, because it is completely unconditional and indestructible. It is simply our true nature—who we actually are before anything else.

> You know who you are, what your life is about, and what you need to do in each moment.

Doing the work laid out on the path of Radical Responsibility can have tremendous results for ourselves and for humanity at large. We're not merely focused on achieving our own ends; this work is grounded in a deep aspiration to reduce suffering and create happiness for all beings. Accordingly, this book is designed structurally to support you in launching and continuing on a path of healing, transformation, and human evolution.

4. DESIGNING AND ESTABLISHING YOUR SADHANA

Sadhana is an ancient Sanskrit word that describes the daily practice, ceremonies, and rituals of a practitioner, or *sadhaka*. Your sadhana becomes the landscape of your daily life and the source that manifests your destiny. It embodies the vision and principles of your chosen path and lays out a clear set of practices and activities designed to promote progress on that path. As a practitioner with a clear life purpose, path, and daily sadhana, you know who you are, what your life is about, and what you need to do in each moment—from the first moment of waking up to the moment you drift off to sleep. One of my mentors talks about our life being like a ceremony or set of rituals, and asserts that it's our particular ceremony that determines our destiny. With that said, let's work on your ceremony.

EXERCISE   Current Ceremony

Start a new section in your Radical Responsibility journal titled "Current Ceremony" and start listing all the activities you engage in each day, working backward over the past week. If the past week was particularly unusual for some reason—say, you were sick or away on vacation—go back a few more weeks and arrive at a clear picture of your usual activities and priorities, intentional or otherwise. That's your ceremony as it stands.

Reflect on it carefully. Ask yourself the following questions: Who designed this ceremony? What are its roots? What will it produce? Where will it take me? In all likelihood, your current ceremony is simply the haphazard creation of your childhood conditioning and life circumstances. Perhaps it entails some useful and even relatively intentional elements, but if you're like most of us, your ceremony was never designed at all—it's simply a routine that keeps you stuck in your ruts, chasing your tail, mindlessly seeking comfort and avoiding discomfort. Reflecting on the reality of your current ceremony, I invite you to take an honest look at whether it will actually manifest the life you want.

EXERCISE   New Transformative Life Ceremony

Create a "New Transformative Life Ceremony" section in your Radical Responsibility journal. In it, design daily routines, practices, rituals, and activities you believe will lead to the results you are looking for. Just get a start on this, as you'll need to come back to it again and again (see "Creating Your Life Plan" later in this chapter). You are beginning to design and establish your sadhana—the daily ceremony that will transform your life and put you on the road to fulfilling your destiny.

5. FINDING YOUR SANGHA, OR COMMUNITY

Sangha is another ancient Sanskrit word in common usage today that describes a community of practitioners focused on supporting each other in spiritual practice and spiritual growth. Finding your spiritual community can be a mysterious process. Of course, you can enjoy fellowship and community with all sorts of diverse groups along the human journey, but your sangha provides a bedrock for your journey and can be one of the greatest sources of joy—and challenge—you'll experience. I encourage you to remain open to the possibility of finding a group like this. Even if you are not a joiner by inclination, your sangha is out there somewhere, and when you find it, you'll know it.

As a spiritual seeker in the late 1960s and early 1970s, I bounced around exploring one tradition after another. I first discovered my sangha and path while living in a remote valley high in the Andes of Peru. A visiting traveler showed up at my home one day in 1974 with a copy of *Rolling Stone* featuring a story on the now legendary first summer sessions at Naropa University with luminaries from the spiritual, philosophical, and avant-garde scenes of that era, including Chögyam Trungpa Rinpoche, Buckminster Fuller, John Cage, and Allen Ginsberg. Reading the article, I felt an urgent call to check out this radical new experiment in higher education. Sitting in my first Naropa class, Intro to Buddhist Psychology, I knew I was finally home. The square peg had found a square hole! Over four decades later, I'm profoundly grateful to have discovered the path and community that is still very much my spiritual home and sangha today.

I share this story to point to the serendipitous nature of finding your sangha, but also to convey a sense of trust. Personally, I feel that if we are open, it will happen sooner or later. As the traditional saying goes, when the student is ready, the teacher appears. A key to recognizing your community is its alignment with and appreciation for your highest purpose, values, and principles. Getting clear about those is a necessary prerequisite to finding your particular path and sangha.

6. CULTIVATING SPIRITUAL FRIENDS, TEACHERS, AND MENTORS

Whether we are religious or not, or whether we consider ourselves to be spiritually oriented or not, life is a spiritual journey and we are spiritual beings. In sociological terms, we describe spirituality and spiritual well-being as having two interrelated dimensions. The first is the experience of connectedness, integration, and wholeness—intrapersonally (within ourselves), interpersonally (with others), and transpersonally (with some transcendent dimension of life, whatever that may be for us). The second dimension entails a sense of meaning and purpose in our lives. When we experience disconnection or isolation, or when life becomes meaningless for us, we call it *spiritual distress*.

Spiritual friendship is a two-way street.

For me, a key strategy for maintaining spiritual health and well-being and progressing along my chosen path is cultivating trusted spiritual friends, teachers, and mentors. Spiritual friends are fellow travelers on this journey with whom we can share our joys and sorrows, our deepest concerns, and our most inspirational dreams. Spiritual friends are Empowerment Zone spiritual warriors doing their own work. We can count on them to see and appreciate our basic goodness and believe in our highest potential. Spiritual friends support us, accompany us, and inspire us along the way. It's also important to remember that spiritual friendship is a two-way street—a mutual connectedness built on shared values and a positive vision for our lives and the future of humanity on this planet.

Spiritual teachers and mentors are unique spiritual friends who have been trained to provide guidance, support, and friendship along the path. It's essential that they be trustworthy and have integrity; they should walk the talk. Of course, they needn't be saints—no one is perfect. However, in seeking a spiritual teacher, trust is paramount, so do your due diligence and keep your eyes wide open, trusting both your heart and your critical intelligence. If something doesn't feel right, it probably isn't. It can be the role of spiritual teachers to challenge and nudge us beyond our comfort zones, but their actions still should be aligned with shared values and principles. If you feel uncomfortable about a spiritual teacher's actions, communicate your discomfort kindly and without blame in a *responsive-relational* (Empowerment Zone) manner. If the teacher is not open to such feedback or to discussing your concerns openly, it's time to move on. You can offer your feedback and hold their highest good in your heart while moving on to relationships more in alignment with your needs.

CONSCIOUS LIVING: LIFE BY DESIGN

It may sound quite romantic to live like an enlightened Zen poet who wanders about with no direction or plan, simply sleeping when they are tired, eating when they are hungry, spontaneously engaging with whatever comes their way in perfect rhythm with the Tao, the natural flow of the universe. Well, this might work for a Zen adept who is truly enlightened, but for most of us it would spell disaster. It would be a formula for abdicating the control and direction of our lives to our childhood conditioning, our habitual patterns, and the world around us.

Remember the bottom-up brain, that supercomputer sitting on our shoulders and running the show unless we are fully awake and engaged with our conscious top-down brain (and, better yet, our heart-mind). Though our own personal supercomputer provides a number of useful programs for walking, talking, riding a bicycle, and so on, it is also the storehouse for generations of faulty programming, unresolved trauma, and fear-based survival strategies of all kinds. Is that really what we want directing our lives?

Then there's the world around us, constantly clamoring for our attention and seducing us into its agendas. More than ever

Program or be programmed.

before, we are bombarded with email, social media, limitless marketing messages, and distractions of all kinds—some of it now generated by algorithms and artificial intelligence. Unless we simply want to succumb to being mindless consumers and victims of every increasingly sophisticated digital manipulation, we need to have a clear design for our lives—for every day and every hour.

You might think that you don't want to live your life in such a controlled way with every moment planned out, that you want to be free. Well, I've got some bad news for you: you're already living a completely scripted life, but you didn't write the script—someone else did. If you've made it this far on the Radical Responsibility journey, you're likely interested in truly becoming the captain of your own ship. This requires assuming responsibility for the day-to-day, hour-to-hour direction of your life. Staying in the driver's seat of our own life requires commitment, motivation, and practice. Our ultimate motivation is answering the call of our destiny—fulfilling our highest life purpose, whatever that may be. In the meantime, a good backup motivation is the realization that we either embrace the responsibility to set the direction of our life or someone else will. In other words, *program or be programmed.*

CREATING YOUR LIFE PLAN

In building a life plan, we look at each significant dimension in our lives. After getting clear about *where we want to be* versus *where we are now*, we then create a concrete plan for closing the gap. Some obvious domains to focus on are:

- physical health and well-being

- relationships and family

- education and learning

- career and livelihood

- financial health and security

- emotional health and well-being

- spiritual growth

- creative pursuits or hobbies

You may want to try my favorite method for creating a life plan, which involves dividing a circle into segments like pieces of a pie, one for each of the most important domains you decide to focus on.

Once you identify and name the pieces of pie in your life plan chart, you then need to decide what a 10 would be on a scale of 1 to 10, with 10 representing your optimal condition or goal. You then assess where you are for each section of the pie chart. Maybe you're a 6 in the health domain and a 4 in the relationship section, and so on. You can then fill in the pie chart using different colors to get a clear picture of where you are. The next step is to prioritize your focus on particular life domains. Certain things always need more attention—relationships, for example. Next, within each domain you

Life Plan

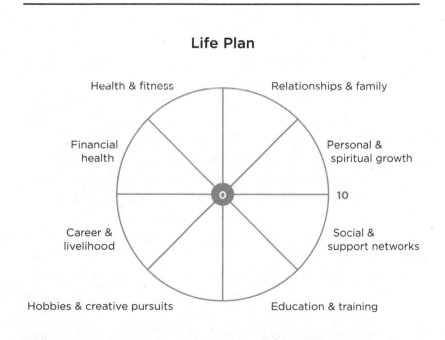

FIGURE 14.1   Life plan pie chart

decide to focus on, develop a plan to get you from where you are now to your optimal condition—that is, a 10.

Your plan needs to be documented with clear timelines and measurable goals. You can get as detailed or broad-stroked with this as you like—just find a way to make it work for you. I'm a visual person, so I have my plan and quarterly goals up on the white board in my office, where I can't avoid it and where I update it regularly. A life plan is a living document, continually changing and evolving, just like us.

FUEL FOR THE JOURNEY—RESILIENCE AND WILLPOWER

Growing and making progress toward fulfilling our highest purpose requires energy. That's why a critical part of our life plan needs to be focused on physical, mental, emotional, and spiritual fitness, health, and resilience. Resilience is often thought of as the ability to bounce back when challenged or knocked down in some way, like a rubber band snapping back after being stretched. One marker of physical resilience is how long it takes our heartbeat to return to baseline after jogging for a period of time. The shorter the time, the more physically fit or resilient we are.

Figure 14.2 offers a simple framework for cultivating different forms of fitness and resilience. This chart is by no means complete or exhaustive, but it will point you in the right direction. Not only is our health and resilience critical to our well-being and quality of life, but it's also the foundation for everything we want to accomplish. Achieving optimal health takes work, but the rewards are more than worth it.

Building up our reservoirs of physical, mental, emotional, and spiritual resilience is like adding batteries to our battery pack and keeping them topped off with regular charging. This requires a plan and, of course, willpower—that elusive combination of motivation and energy that allows us to follow through on our commitments and get things done. I'm going to share a little secret with you here—whatever willpower is, we have a lot more of it first thing in the morning, and it wanes as the day progresses.

You probably know this from experience. Even for those of us who are just not morning people—a completely rewireable habitual pattern,

Physical	Emotional
• Optimize nutrition & hydration	• Practice good listening skills
• Breathe properly—oxygenation	• Develop emotional intelligence
• Exercise regularly	• Manage emotional triggers
• Get enough sleep & rest	• Cultivate emotional resilience
• Limit alcohol & caffeine use	• Maintain healthy relationships
• Eliminate nicotine or other harmful drugs	• Build your support team
	• Work with a mentor/coach
Mental	**Spiritual**
• Practice mindfulness meditation regularly	• Cultivate faith & spirituality
• Cultivate a positive attitude/reframe negative thinking	• Participate in fellowship & community
• Challenge your brain with new learning, languages, games, etc.	• Practice gratitude, forgiveness & letting go
• Expose your mind to positive ideas—books, films, classes, etc.	• Spend time in nature or other enriching activities
	• Volunteer—community service

FIGURE 14.2 Four areas for cultivating fitness and resilience

by the way—we simply have more energy and willpower in the morning than at any other time of day, especially if we get a good night's sleep. Therefore, an ideal place to begin implementing a new design for your life is with your morning routines. I highly recommend using the first hour or two of the day to attend to hygiene, mindfulness meditation practice, physical exercise, and nutrition to set you up for an optimal day. After that, you're primed and ready to spend the next several hours tackling the toughest tasks of your day.

BRINGING IT ALL HOME

If you have read this far, you likely have some degree of trust in your own innate basic goodness, or you're at least open to the possibility. Ultimately, we can't really make a mistake on this journey—everything we encounter is another opportunity to learn. At the same time, on the relational level we do make mistakes that negatively impact others and ourselves. However, none of these mistakes, no matter how egregious, are any indication of unworthiness or a flaw of some kind in our basic nature. If we view them as simply speed bumps, they can actually help us reawaken to our commitment to evolve as an accountable, ethical, and compassionate human being. Living in the Empowerment Zone, we clean up our mistakes with others and make amends where appropriate and possible. We also learn to forgive ourselves and generate compassion for ourselves and others using the practices we explored in chapter 13.

Remembering that circumstances are neutral, we can always stop, breathe, take a fresh look at our circumstances, no matter where we find ourselves, and ask that magical question: "What can I do?" Again and again, we make the courageous shift from fear and survival to freedom and possibility. Over time, we learn to embody the domain of Authentic Relationship and navigate life with openhearted awareness and genuineness—the awakened heart-mind.

While moments of clarity, transcendence, and joy are, of course, wonderful when they happen, you are likely already aware that our most profound insights and growth often arise out of challenge and suffering. By contemplating the mental models offered in this book and fully engaging in the various practices found here, you are embarking on a new path and challenging yourself in new ways. So be prepared to fall off the horse. And then be prepared to fall off the horse again. Simply commit yourself to climbing back in the saddle every time without fail. Over time, it gets easier—the falls are less painful and less frequent as you learn to hold your seat and ride the energy of life's ever-changing challenges.

May the wind be ever at your back. And may you meet with abundant success along the path of Radical Responsibility as you move beyond blame, fearlessly live your highest purpose, and become an unstoppable force for good.

NOTES

INTRODUCTION

1. Rich Simon, "A Q&A with Tony Robbins: What's His Message for Therapists?" *Psychotherapy Networker*, December 4, 2017, psychotherapynetworker.org/blog/details/1355/a-qa-with-tony-robbins.

CHAPTER 2: THE POWER OF PRESENCE

1. Chögyam Trungpa, *Shambhala: The Sacred Path of the Warrior* (Boulder, CO: Shambhala Publications, 1984), 107.
2. Matthew A. Killingsworth and Daniel T. Gilbert, "A Wandering Mind Is an Unhappy Mind," *Science* 330, no. 6006 (November 12, 2010): 932, doi.org/10.1126/science.1192439.
3. Yi-Yuang Tang, Britta K. Hölzel, and Michael I. Posner, "The Neuroscience of Mindfulness Meditation," *Nature Reviews Neuroscience* 16, no. 4 (April 2015): 213–25, doi.org/10.1038/nrn3916.
4. Jon Kabat-Zinn, *Wherever You Go, There You Are: Mindfulness Meditation in Everyday Life* (New York: Hyperion, 1994), 4.
5. G. Alan Marlatt and Jean L. Kristeller, "Mindfulness and Meditation," in *Integrating Spirituality into Treatment: Resources for Practitioners*, ed. William R. Miller (Washington, DC: American Psychological Association, 1999), 67–84, doi.org/10.1037/10327-004.
6. Chögyam Trungpa, *Shambhala*, 75.
7. Daniel J. Siegel, "Mindfulness Training and Neural Integration: Differentiation of Distinct Streams of Awareness and the Cultivation of Well-Being," *Social Cognitive and Affective Neuroscience* 2, no. 4 (December 2007): 259–63, doi.org/10.1093/scan/nsm034.

CHAPTER 3: THE POWER OF EMPATHIC AWARENESS

1. Steven J. Stein et al., "Emotional Intelligence of Leaders: A Profile of Top Executives," *Leadership & Organization Development Journal* 30, no. 1 (February 2009): 87–101, doi.org/10.1108/01437730910927115.
2. Daniel Goleman, "What Makes a Leader?" *Harvard Business Review*, January 1, 2004, hbr.org/2004/01/what-makes-a-leader.

3. Daniel Goleman, *Emotional Intelligence: Why It Can Matter More Than IQ* (New York: Bantam, 1995).

4. Henry S. Randall, *The Life of Thomas Jefferson*, vol. 3 (New York: Derby & Jackson, 1858), 525.

5. David Rock, "SCARF: A Brain-Based Model for Collaborating with and Influencing Others," *NeuroLeadership Journal*, no. 1 (2008): 1–9, epa.gov/sites/production/files/2015-09/documents/thurs _georgia_9_10_915_covello.pdf.

6. Olga M. Klimecki et al., "Differential Pattern of Functional Brain Plasticity after Compassion and Empathy Training," *Social Cognitive and Affective Neuroscience* 9, no. 6 (June 2014): 873–79, doi.org/10.1093/scan/nst060; Olga M. Klimecki and Tania Singer, "Empathic Distress Fatigue Rather Than Compassion Fatigue? Integrating Findings from Empathy Research in Psychology and Social Neuroscience," in *Pathological Altruism*, ed. Barbara Oakley et al. (New York: Oxford University Press, 2012), doi.org/10.1093 /acprof:oso/9780199738571.003.0253.

CHAPTER 4: THE HUMAN CONDITION—A FRAGILE BEGINNING

1. Steven Pinker, *The Better Angels of Our Nature: Why Violence Has Declined* (New York: Penguin, 2012).

CHAPTER 5: STUCK ON THE DRAMA TRIANGLE AGAIN

1. Stephen Karpman, "Fairy Tales and Script Drama Analysis," *Transactional Analysis Bulletin* 7, no. 26 (1968): 39–43.

2. Matthew White, "Necrometrics: Estimated Totals for the Entire 20th Century," *Historical Atlas of the 20th Century*, last updated September 2010, necrometrics.com/all20c.htm.

CHAPTER 6: GETTING OFF THE DRAMA TRIANGLE

1. Pema Chödrön, *Don't Bite the Hook: Finding Freedom from Anger, Resentment, and Other Destructive Emotions*, read by Pema Chödrön (Boston: Shambhala Audio, 2007).

CHAPTER 7: TAKING CHARGE OF YOUR DESTINY— BRAIN SCIENCE 101

1. Herbert Benson with Miriam Z. Klipper, *The Relaxation Response*, updated and expanded edition (New York: William Morrow, 2000).

2. Paul D. MacLean, *The Triune Brain in Evolution: Role in Paleocerebral Functions* (New York: Plenum Press, 1990).

3. Daniel Goleman, *Emotional Intelligence: Why It Can Matter More Than IQ* (New York: Bantam, 1995).

4. Abiola Keller et al., "Does the Perception that Stress Affects Health Matter? The Association with Health and Mortality," *Health Psychology* 31, no. 5 (September 2012): 677–84, doi.org/10.1037 /a0026743.

5. Kelly McGonigal, *The Upside of Stress: Why Stress Is Good for You, and How to Get Good at It* (New York: Penguin Random House, 2016).

CHAPTER 8: RUTS AND GROOVES— REWIRING THE BRAIN FOR SUCCESS

1. Daniel Goleman, *Focus: The Hidden Driver of Excellence* (New York: HarperCollins, 2013).

2. Kirsten Hötting and Brigette Röder, "Beneficial Effects of Physical Exercise on Neuroplacticity and Cognition," *Neuroscience & Biobehavioral Reviews* 37, no. 9b (November 2013): 2243–57, doi.org/10.1016/j.neubiorev.2013.04.005; Britta K. Hölzel et al., "Mindfulness Practice Leads to Increases in Regional Brain Gray Matter Density," *Psychiatry Research* 191, no. 1 (January 2011): 36–43, doi.org/10.1016/j.pscychresns.2010.08.006; Micah Allen et al., "Cognitive-Affective Neural Plasticity Following Active-Controlled Mindfulness Intervention," *Journal of Neuroscience* 32, no. 44 (October 2012): 15601–10, doi.org/10.1523/JNEUROSCI.2957-12.2012.

3. Michelle W. Voss et al., "Exercise, Brain, and Cognition across the Life Span," *Journal of Applied Physiology* 111, no. 5 (November 2011): 1505–13, doi.org/10.1152/japplphysiol.00210.2011; Louis Bherer, Kirk I. Erickson, and Teresa Liu-Ambrose, "A Review of the Effects of Physical Activity and Exercise on Cognitive and Brain Functions in Older Adults," *Journal of Aging Research* 2013 (2013): article 657508, doi.org/10.1155/2013/657508; Karlene Ball et al., "Effects of Cognitive Training Interventions with Older Adults: A Randomized Controlled Trial," *JAMA: Journal of the American Medical Association* 288, no. 18 (November 13, 2002): 2271–81, doi.org/10.1001/jama.288.18.2271.

4. M. J. Dauncey, "Recent Advances in Nutrition, Genes and Brain Health," *Proceedings of the Nutrition Society* 71, no. 4 (November

2012): 581–91, doi: 10.1017/S0029665112000237; Natalie
Parletta, Catherine M. Milte, and Barbara J. Meyer, "Nutritional
Modulation of Cognitive Function and Mental Health," *Journal of
Nutritional Biochemistry* 24, no. 5 (May 2013): 725–43,
doi.org/10.1016/j.jnutbio.2013.01.002.

5. Rinske A. Gotink et al., "8-Week Mindfulness Based Stress
Reduction Induces Brain Changes Similar to Traditional Long-Term
Meditation Practice—a Systematic Review," *Brain and Cognition*
108 (October 2016): 32–41, doi.org/10.1016/j.bandc.2016.07.001;
William R. Marchand, "Neural Mechanisms of Mindfulness and
Meditation: Evidence from Neuroimaging Studies," *World Journal
of Radiology* 6, no. 7 (July 28, 2014): 471–79, doi.org/10.4329/wjr
.v6.i7.471; Maddalena Boccia, Laura Piccardi, and Paola Guariglia,
"The Meditative Mind: A Comprehensive Meta-Analysis of MRI
Studies," *BioMed Research International* (June 2015): article 419808,
doi.org/10.1155/2015/419808.

6. Phillippa Lally et al., "How Are Habits Formed: Modelling Habit
Formation in the Real World," *European Journal of Social Psychology*
40, no. 6 (October 2010): 998–1009, doi.org/10.1002/ejsp.674.

7. Boccia, Piccardi, and Guariglia, "The Meditative Mind."

8. Yi-Yuan Tang, Rongxiang Tang, and Michael I. Posner,
"Mindfulness Meditation Improves Emotion Regulation
and Reduces Drug Abuse," *Drug and Alcohol Dependence* 163,
no. S1 (June 1, 2016): S13–18, doi.org/10.1016/j
.drugalcdep.2015.11.041; Gotink et al., "8-Week Mindfulness Based
Stress Reduction," 32–41.

9. Daniel Goleman and Richard Davidson, *Altered Traits: Science
Reveals How Meditation Changes Your Mind, Brain, and Body*
(New York: Avery, 2017).

CHAPTER 10: THE NATURE OF CIRCUMSTANCES

1. Marcus Aurelius, *Meditations*, trans. Gregory Hays (New York:
Modern Library, 2002).

2. Bodhipaksa, "Esther Lederer: 'Hanging onto resentment is letting
someone you despise live rent-free in your head,'" *Wildmind* (blog),
October 31, 2007, wildmind.org/blogs/quote-of-the-month
/ann-landers-resentment.

3. "Resentment Is Like Taking Poison and Waiting for the
Other Person to Die," Quote Investigator, August 19, 2017,
quoteinvestigator.com/2017/08/19/resentment.

CHAPTER 11: DISCOVERING AUTHENTIC RELATIONSHIP

1. Fred Luskin, *Forgive for Good: A Proven Prescription for Health and Happiness* (San Francisco: HarperSanFrancisco, 2001).
2. Chögyam Trungpa, *Shambhala: The Sacred Path of the Warrior* (Boulder, CO: Shambhala Publications, 1984).

CHAPTER 12: THE EMPOWERMENT TRIANGLE
AND RADICAL POSSIBILITY

1. David Emerald, *The Power of TED** *(*The Empowerment Dynamic): The Key to Creating an Extraordinary Life* (Bainbridge Island, WA: Polaris Publishing, 2006).
2. Adapted from the work of Rick Hanson, PhD; used with permission.
3. Pema Chödrön, *Start Where You Are: A Guide to Compassionate Living* (Boston: Shambhala Publications, 1994).
4. Carlos Castaneda, *The Fire from Within* (New York: Simon & Schuster, 1984).

CHAPTER 13: DISCOVERING THE POWER
OF COMPASSION AND RESILIENCE

1. Emma M. Seppälä, "Compassion: Our First Instinct," *Psychology Today*, June 03, 2013, psychologytoday.com/us/blog /feeling-it/201306/compassion-our-first-instinct.
2. Tenzin Gyatso, His Holiness the 14th Dalai Lama of Tibet, "Compassion and the Individual," accessed November 10, 2018, dalailama.com/messages/compassion-and-human-values /compassion.
3. Daniel J. Siegel, *Mindsight: The New Science of Personal Transformation* (New York: Bantam, 2010).
4. Daniel J. Siegel, *Aware: The Science and Practice of Presence* (New York: TarcherPerigree, 2018).
5. Emma M. Seppällä, "18 Science-Backed Reasons to Try Loving-Kindness Meditation!" *Psychology Today*, September 15, 2014, psychologytoday.com/us/blog/feeling-it/201409/18-science-backed -reasons-try-loving-kindness-meditation.
6. Seppällä, "18 Science-Backed Reasons to Try Loving-Kindness Meditation!"
7. James N. Kirby, "Compassion Interventions: The Programmes, the Evidence, and Implications for Research and Practice,"

Psychology and Psychotherapy: Theory, Research and Practice 90, no. 3 (September 2016): 432–55, doi.org/10.1111/papt.12104; Julieta Galante et al., "Effect of Kindness-Based Meditation on Health and Well-Being: A Systematic Review and Meta-Analysis," *Journal of Consulting and Clinical Psychology* 82, no. 6 (December 2014): 1101–14, doi.org/10.1037/a0037249; Hooria Jazaieri et al., "Enhancing Compassion: A Randomized Controlled Trial of a Compassion Cultivation Training Program," *Journal of Happiness Studies* 14, no. 4 (August 2013): 1113–26, doi.org/10.1007 /s10902-012-9373-z; Stefan G. Hofmann, Paul Grossman, and Devon E. Hinton, "Loving-Kindness and Compassion Meditation: Potential for Psychological Interventions," *Clinical Psychology Review* 31, no. 7 (November 2011): 1126–32, doi.org/10.1016/j .cpr.2011.07.003.

8. Daniel J. Siegel, "Mindful Awareness, Mindsight, and Neural Integration," *Humanistic Psychologist* 37, no. 2 (April–June 2009): 137–58, doi.org/10.1080/08873260902892220; Daniel J. Siegel, *The Developing Mind: How Relationships and the Brain Interact to Shape Who We Are*, second edition (New York: Guilford Publications, 2012); Daniel J. Siegel, *Mind: A Journey to the Heart of Being Human* (New York: W. W. Norton, 2016).

9. Daniel Goleman and Richard J. Davidson, *Altered Traits: Science Reveals How Meditation Changes Your Mind, Brain, and Body* (New York: Avery, 2017).

10. Daniel J. Siegel, "Me + We = Mwe," YouTube, filmed at Omega Institute, posted February 8, 2016, video, 1:29, youtube.com /watch?v=uo8Yo4UE6g0.

11. Daniel J. Siegel, *Mindsight: The New Science of Personal Transformation* (New York: Bantam, 2010); Siegel, *Mind*.

12. Abraham Lincoln, "First Inaugural Address" (speech, Est Portico, United States Capitol, Washington, DC, March 4, 1861), accessed November 10, 2018, avalon.law.yale.edu/19th_century/lincoln1.asp.

ADDITIONAL RESOURCES FOR YOUR PATH

Allione, Tsultrim. *Feeding Your Demons: Ancient Wisdom for Resolving Inner Conflict.* New York: Little, Brown, 2008.

Arendt, Hannah. *The Human Condition.* Second edition. Chicago: University of Chicago Press, 1998.

Aurelius, Marcus. *Meditations.* Translated by Gregory Hays. New York: Modern Library, 2002.

Brown, Brené. *Daring Greatly: How the Courage to Be Vulnerable Transforms the Way We Live, Love, Parent, and Lead.* New York: Avery, 2015.

Chödrön, Pema. *Don't Bite the Hook: Finding Freedom from Anger, Resentment, and Other Destructive Emotions.* Boston: Shambhala Audio, 2007. 3 CDs, 3 hr., 30 min.

Chödrön, Pema. *Taking the Leap: Freeing Ourselves from Old Habits and Fears.* Boston: Shambhala Publications, 2009.

Dalio, Ray. *Principles: Life and Work.* New York: Simon & Schuster, 2017.

Duhigg, Charles. *The Power of Habit: Why We Do What We Do in Life and Business.* New York: Random House, 2012.

Dweck, Carol S. *Mindset: The New Psychology of Success.* Updated edition. New York: Ballantine, 2007.

Emerald, David. *The Power of TED* (*The Empowerment Dynamic): The Key to Creating an Extraordinary Life.* Bainbridge Island, WA: Polaris Publishing, 2006.

Glassman, Bernie. *Bearing Witness: A Zen Master's Lessons in Making Peace.* New York: Harmony, 1998.

Goleman, Daniel. *Emotional Intelligence: Why It Can Matter More Than IQ.* New York: Bantam, 1995.

Goleman, Daniel, and Richard J. Davidson. *Altered Traits: Science Reveals How Meditation Changes Your Mind, Brain, and Body.* New York: Avery, 2017.

Halifax, Joan. *Standing at the Edge: Finding Freedom Where Fear and Courage Meet.* New York: Flatiron Books, 2018.

Hanson, Rick. *Buddha's Brain: The Practical Neuroscience of Happiness, Love & Wisdom.* Oakland, CA: New Harbinger, 2009.

Hebb, Donald O. *The Organization of Behavior: A Neuropsychological Theory.* New York: John Wiley & Sons, 1949.

Howard, Jane. "Doom and Glory of Knowing Who You Are." *Life* 54, no. 21 (May 24, 1963): 89.

Kabat-Zinn, Jon. *Arriving at Your Own Door: 108 Lessons in Mindfulness.* New York: Hyperion, 2007.

Kabat-Zinn, Jon. *Full Catastrophe Living: Using the Wisdom of Your Body and Mind to Face Stress, Pain, and Illness.* Revised edition. New York: Bantam, 2013.

Kabat-Zinn, Jon. *Wherever You Go, There You Are: Mindfulness Meditation in Everyday Life.* New York: Hyperion, 1994.

Katie, Byron. *Loving What Is: Four Questions That Can Change Your Life.* New York: Harmony, 2002.

Leonard, George. *Mastery: The Keys to Success and Long-Term Fulfillment.* New York: Dutton, 1991.

Lozowick, Lee. *The Alchemy of Transformation.* Prescott, AZ: Hohm Press, 1996.

Manson, Mark. *The Subtle Art of Not Giving a F*ck: A Counterintuitive Approach to Living a Good Life.* New York: HarperCollins, 2016.

Maraboli, Steve. *Unapologetically You: Reflections on Life and the Human Experience.* Port Washington, NY: A Better Today Publishing, 2013.

Mayer, John D., and Peter Salovey. "What Is Emotional Intelligence?" In *Emotional Development and Emotional Intelligence: Educational Implications,* edited by Peter Salovey and David J. Sluyter, 3–31. New York: Basic Books, 1997.

McGonigal, Kelly. *The Willpower Instinct: How Self-Control Works, Why It Matters, and What You Can Do to Get More of It.* New York: Avery, 2012.

Mingyur, Yongey. "Lasting Happiness." *Lion's Roar,* January 19, 2012. lionsroar.com/lasting-happiness-march-2012.

Mipham, Sakyong. *Ruling Your World: Ancient Strategies for Modern Life.* New York: Morgan Road, 2005.

Mipham, Sakyong. *Turning the Mind Into an Ally.* New York: Riverhead, 2003.

Murray, W. H. *The Scottish Himalayan Expedition.* London: J. M. Dent, 1951.

Ramón y Cajal, Santiago. *Recollections of My Life.* Translated by E. Horne Craigie and Juan Cano. Boston: MIT Press, 1989.

Richo, David. *How to Be an Adult: A Handbook on Psychological and Spiritual Integration.* Mahwah, NJ: Paulist Press, 1991.

Robbins, Tony. *Awaken the Giant Within: How to Take Immediate Control of Your Mental, Emotional, Physical and Financial Destiny.* New York: Simon & Schuster, 1991.

Robbins, Tony. *Unlimited Power: The New Science of Personal Achievement.* New York: Simon & Schuster, 1986.

Ruiz, don Miguel. *The Four Agreements: A Practical Guide to Personal Freedom.* San Rafael, CA: Amber-Allen Publishing, 1997.

Salzberg, Sharon. *Lovingkindness: The Revolutionary Art of Happiness.* Boston: Shambhala Publications, 1995.

Seng-Ts'an. *Hsin-Hsin Ming: Verses on the Faith Mind.* Translated by Richard Clarke. Buffalo, NY: White Pine Press, 1984.

Siegel, Daniel J. *Mind: A Journey to the Heart of Being Human.* New York: W. W. Norton, 2016.

Siegel, Daniel J. *Mindsight: The New Science of Personal Transformation.* New York: Bantam, 2010.

Siegel, Daniel J. "The Self Is Not Defined by the Boundaries of Our Skin." *Psychology Today*, February 28, 2014. psychologytoday.com/us/blog /inspire-rewire/201402/the-self-is-not-defined-the-boundaries-our-skin.

Stanton, Brandon. *Humans of New York*. New York: St. Martin's Press, 2013.

Tan, Chade-Meng. *Search Inside Yourself: The Unexpected Path of Achieving Success, Happiness (and World Peace)*. New York: HarperOne, 2012.

Tolle, Eckhart. *The Power of Now: A Guide to Spiritual Enlightenment*. Novato, CA: New World Library, 1999.

Trungpa, Chögyam. *Shambhala: The Sacred Path of the Warrior*. Boulder, CO: Shambhala Publications, 1984.

Trungpa, Chögyam. *Smile at Fear: Awakening the True Heart of Bravery*. Edited by Carolyn Rose Gimian. Boston: Shambhala Publications, 2010.

Williamson, Marianne. *A Return to Love: Reflections on the Principles of "A Course in Miracles."* New York: HarperCollins, 1992.

ABOUT THE AUTHOR

Fleet Maull, PhD, is a meditation teacher, social entrepreneur, executive coach, and global changemaker who leads meditation and bearing witness retreats, leadership trainings, prison programs, and personal evolution seminars around the world.

He is a grateful survivor of the counterculture revolution of the 1960s and 1970s and his early travels and adventures throughout Central and South America. He founded two national organizations, Prison Mindfulness Institute and National Prison Hospice Association, while serving a fourteen-year drug sentence (1985–1999) at a maximum security federal prison. After his release, Fleet also cofounded the Engaged Mindfulness Institute and Windhorse Hill Retreat Center in Deerfield, Massachusetts, the Buddhist Chaplaincy Training Program at the Upaya Zen Center in Santa Fe, New Mexico, and the Rwanda Bearing Witness Retreat and Peace Initiative.

Fleet is a fully-empowered senior Dharma teacher in both the Zen and Tibetan Buddhist meditation traditions. He is a *roshi* (Zen master) and Dharma successor of Roshi Bernie Glassman in the Soto Zen lineage and Zen Peacemaker Order. He is also an *acharya* (senior Dharma teacher) in the Tibetan Buddhist tradition and a longtime senior student of the renowned meditation master Chögyam Trungpa Rinpoche. He is an International Mindfulness Teachers Association (IMTA) certified professional mindfulness teacher. He taught Buddhist psychology, socially engaged Buddhism, and contemplative social action and peacemaking at Naropa University for ten years (1999–2009) and often presents at other universities and colleges such as Harvard, Brown, Emory, University of Colorado, and Smith. He is a frequent conference presenter on topics related to mindfulness, emotional intelligence, leadership, and criminal justice. Fleet is the author of *Dharma in Hell: The Prison Writings of Fleet Maull* and numerous book chapters and journal articles in the mindfulness, hospice, and criminal justice fields.

He lives with his partner, Sophie, in a small town in western Massachusetts, where they wake up each morning to the sun rising over the Connecticut River. For more information, please visit fleetmaull.com.

ABOUT SOUNDS TRUE

Sounds True is a multimedia publisher whose mission is to inspire and support personal transformation and spiritual awakening. Founded in 1985 and located in Boulder, Colorado, we work with many of the leading spiritual teachers, thinkers, healers, and visionary artists of our time. We strive with every title to preserve the essential "living wisdom" of the author or artist. It is our goal to create products that not only provide information to a reader or listener, but that also embody the quality of a wisdom transmission.

For those seeking genuine transformation, Sounds True is your trusted partner. At SoundsTrue.com you will find a wealth of free resources to support your journey, including exclusive weekly audio interviews, free downloads, interactive learning tools, and other special savings on all our titles.

To learn more, please visit SoundsTrue.com/freegifts or call us toll-free at 800.333.9185.

sounds true
WAKING UP THE WORLD